4 5/1

D0894931

CAMBRIDGE, U.S.A.

CAMBRIDGE, U.S.A.

HUB OF A NEW WORLD

BY CHRISTOPHER RAND

F
74
CIR3

NEW YORK

OXFORD UNIVERSITY PRESS · 1964

35915

Copyright © 1964 by Christopher Rand
Library of Congress Catalogue Card Number: 64-24865

The material in this book appeared originally in *The New Yorker*
in somewhat shorter form; © 1964 by The New Yorker Magazine, Inc.

PRINTED IN THE UNITED STATES OF AMERICA

To my family

ACKNOWLEDGMENTS

This whole work was undertaken by *The New Yorker* and me together, and without *The New Yorker* it could not have been done.

I have also been helped by innumerable friends in Cambridge and elsewhere. I cannot list them—nor would they all want me to—but they know what they did for me, and I trust they know how thankful I am.

C.R.

CONTENTS

CAMBRIDGE, U.S.A.

ROUTE 128

I SOME MONTHS AGO I came back to live in Cambridge, Mass., after a fourteen-year absence, and at once I found changes afoot. I saw new defense plants that had shot up in Cambridge and its environs, attracted by the scientists of M.I.T. I saw more Indians, Africans, and other strangers in town than I had seen of old, and I learned that the Cambridge professors themselves were more global in their interests; they were orbiting round the world more and exerting more influence on foreign lands. They seemed to have more scope. Then as the weeks passed, and I slipped back into my old groove, I learned that some of the social sciences were also booming: that a combination of new money and new technology had given them a new hold on life, and a new approach to it.

Soon I decided that I had found a renaissance in Cambridge, as I shall try to explain. Like any renaissance it has its special features. It has its patrons, its Medici, in the faceless U.S. government and the great impersonal foundations; all the changes I have mentioned depend on funds from them. Again it has a bent for research, as opposed to teaching, and for group research at that; its savants are usually banded in teams, working on complex projects that cut across the old academic disciplines. These teams are sometimes housed in defense plants — making missiles, say, or warning-nets — and sometimes in new institutions called centers, which have sprouted from the universities themselves. Either way they have a semi-free existence, and nearly always they are run by leaders of a new type: by academic entrepreneurs, who are men of affairs as well as learning — who know how to raise money, and put an organization together, and get results in the outside world. They do their work in a mood of urgency — of urgency to make new weapons, to solve our foreign problems, or to doctor up our social health. Driven thus by our *malaises,* the renaissance is pushing knowledge ahead here furiously while much altering some parts of the academic life (not all parts, though, be it said; the treatment of the arts and letters, for instance, by Cambridge and its world is hardly changed).

I should explain what I mean by Cambridge and its world. Only the center of that world lies in Cambridge proper — in the grounds of Harvard and M.I.T., these being a mile apart, on the north bank of the Charles as that river flows eastward to Boston Harbor. Boston itself, on the Charles's *south* bank, is much penetrated by the Cambridge world, and then just north of Cambridge there is Tufts, while a few miles west of it there is Brandeis. Both these universities are in the movement too, Brandeis being one of its newest features. It barely existed when I lived here fourteen years ago. I used to walk out that way sometimes on a Sunday; the trip would take a few hours, going up the Charles. Brandeis then consisted of little more than a grotesque old turreted castle on a hill; I never realized what it was. But now the castle has been joined by countless new, rectangular buildings made of brick, glass, and concrete. They are rather jammed together on their rise of ground, but they are *chic* and modern-looking, very much a part of the new era.

Just west of Brandeis one comes to Route 128, another of the era's key parts. Route 128 hardly existed, either, in my former sojourn, which took place in the school year 1948–49. My choice of that moment had nothing to do, consciously, with this present report, yet the year does make a good base-line for it, as few of the trends I am noting were then visible. The Korean War was unthought of in 1948–49 (at least by us Americans), and so were Sputnik, the Russian nuclear threat, and the other alarms now spurring us on. It was a moment when peace could be viewed as a normal state, and a moment, too, when our civilian production, long dammed up, was ready to burst forth. Our building industry had been in the doldrums since the early 'thirties, and our production of consumer goods had been in them since Pearl Harbor. We were cramped with shortages and demanding that they cease.

All this came to bear, in time, on 128's development, but at first the route was just a simple expression of highway theory; it was a "ring road" designed to keep long-distance traffic out of Boston. It describes a semicircle round the city, some ten miles from its heart, with both ends resting on or near the shores of Massachusetts Bay (to make a full circle around Boston, a road would have to be amphibious). Thanks to 128 a car can be deflected from one part to another of the Boston hinterland — from the quarter of Maine, say, to that of western Massachusetts or Cape Cod — without losing speed or further congesting the city. The road's building, at the start, was much criticized; Massachusetts was in a slump then, taxes were high, and the textile mills were fleeing southward; inevitably 128 was damned as an extravagance of the politicians. Yet it was built, and since then it has hummed.*

Around the time it was finished, a dozen years ago, business firms of certain types had begun leaving the core of Boston (as of other American cities) for the outskirts. One reason was that these firms could finally build new plants, after two decades of waiting. Another was that downtown traffic jams were becoming too much for them. And a third was that new ways of moving and storing objects within buildings had developed. Instead of moving them up and down by elevators, the tendency was now to move them horizontally by fork-lifts and similar vehicles. This called for wide-spreading structures rather than high-rising ones, and hence for more space, which could not be had in the city's heart. According to experts in Cabot, Cabot & Forbes, the real-estate firm that has masterminded the exodus here, these three pressures were felt most heavily, at first, by companies that operated warehouses — by the New England distributors, say, of goods produced on a national scale. In the past such companies had been wedded to the city's core, but in 1948 C.,C.&F. lured several of them, including the local establishments of General Electric, Squibb, and Parke-Davis, to the "suburbs." Actually this first move was a timid one, just across the Charles from downtown Boston to East Cambridge. But three or four years later C.,C.&F. settled a few other firms in *West* Cambridge, half-way to

---

* Recently 128 has been widened for its increased traffic. This has been tremendously expensive because the road's bridges and overpasses were not originally built to allow for it.

Route 128, and soon they were putting still others on 128 itself.

By this time, light-manufacturing companies and mere offices were joining the parade, and C.,C.&F. was housing them in industrial parks, another new feature of our century; industrial parks are business areas laid out in open country and governed much like residential tracts — the tenants, that is, agree to build on only so much of their land, to plant the rest attractively, and otherwise to observe the amenities. C.,C.&F. (and a few other real-estate firms) began establishing these parks along 128 and erecting non-committal, oblong, one-story buildings in them, which could then be rented, as a multiple unit or separately, to a mixed bag of clients. And thus they prepared a way for the defense industries to come.

The Cambridge scientific world had been active industrially in the Hitler war, developing radar and other devices. Then had come a lull — with the electronics business staying alive, though, because of things like TV and the deep freeze — and then finally, in the late 'fifties, the space-and-missile boom brought more activity than ever. The Cambridge area (as I learned in my investigation) specializes in small plants making "sophisticated" items — under the guidance of scientists and engineers from the local universities — and that specialty has been found invaluable in the supplying of electronic components for space vehicles. M.I.T. has always led overwhelmingly in such practical endeavors here, and scores of the new wonder-firms have "spun off" from the Institute, their inventions having been made either in M.I.T. laboratories themselves or in lofts in the Cambridge industrial warrens nearby. Many a shoe-string firm, with little capital other than M.I.T. brains, has begun in these warrens. If it has shown promise it has picked up financing — perhaps old Boston money from State Street — and moved to better surroundings. And since the late 'fifties this has meant, pre-eminently, moving to 128, where the firm can get what it needs for its next phase: an adaptable new building; good access to highways; lots of parking space; and a pleasant landscape for its scientists to contemplate. It also gets access to like enterprises there — to their products and know-how — and it gets prestige; the arrival of an electronics firm on 128 (one hears in Cambridge) is now like the arrival of a store on Fifth Avenue; its sales and stock-value go up at once.

In the past few years 128 has come to have a legendary name, being called simply "the Road" by its habitués and things like "the Space Highway" and "the Golden Semicircle" by the business press. It has also come to have a distinctive, rather puzzling appearance. It is a modern superhighway with many lanes, no stoplights,* and frequent overpasses where it is crossed by radial roads fanning out from Boston. The motorist whizzes along it flanked, for the most part, by country landscape, broken here and there by long, low mysterious buildings flaunting cryptic names like Itek, Tracerlab Keleket, Tech Weld, Sylvania, and Raytheon. Not only a man from Mars would be puzzled by 128. A man from almost anywhere would.

When I began exploring the Cambridge renaissance I toured 128 with two expert guides, R. John Griefen and Daniel Wheeler, who are both officers of Cabot, Cabot & Forbes. (C.,C.&F., they told me, has helped establish more than half the "research-and-development" companies now on 128 — research and development, or R & D, being a

---

* Actually there is one stoplight near 128's northeastern end.

technical term for the seeking out of new materials or devices and the engineering of practical ways to make them.) *

Griefen and Wheeler picked me up late one morning in a station-wagon, near Harvard Square, and soon we were speeding off through the suburbs of West Cambridge. "The land is all built up through here," said Griefen, who was driving. "That's one reason why 128 is so successful. It passes through the open country nearest to Boston. There's no room in here for building, but there's lots out there." We went on through the suburbs, which were drab — now we ran the gauntlet between two-family houses, now we flashed by gas-stations and shops — always we made our way through urban sprawl. "The real selling-point of 128," said Griefen, "is the landscape there. The research-and-development industry depends almost wholly on scientists and engineers. A firm must be able to attract and hold them, perhaps lure them from other firms. It can't do this by money alone, for in the end most firms will pay about the same for men of equal ability, so it does it by offering nice surroundings. A scientist likes a quiet office with a blackboard, a window, and a tree outside, and it is better still if the tree has a squirrel in it. Route 128 supplies that kind of thing."

We reached 128 in fifteen or twenty minutes and dropped down to it, by a cloverleaf, from the radial we had been on. We merged with the 128 traffic and spun along amid sunny fall weather. The landscape was of a kind one often sees near Boston — slightly rolling and covered by

* Gerald W. Blakeley, head of C.,C.&F., is the main initiator of industrial parks in the Boston region and has also been operating on a national scale; his firm has established two dozen parks across the U.S. — from New England to the West Coast — by now.

expanses of pink grass interspersed with oak thickets; the oak-leaves were dead and brown now, in October, but still hanging from the branches. "We'll go first to Clevite," said Griefen. "Our firm designed their plant, a few years ago, and we got a prize for it. Clevite is a Cleveland company; they make transistors. A few years ago they decided to expand — to get into a better research-and-development area — but they didn't know just where to go. So they polled some twenty-two hundred scientists throughout the country, asking their preference. The scientists declared about equally for here and the San Francisco Bay region, so Clevite built in each."

The Clevite plant, when we got to it, was a two-story affair with planes of metal-framed windows interrupted by planes of stone masonry, the latter warm in tone. It stood back from the road amid vegetation that would have graced a fine suburban villa; the landscaping, my guides told me, had been done by Professor Hideo Sasaki of Harvard, a well-known master. We drove round to the building's rear, parked, got out, and had a look. There was a luxurious lawn there, punctuated by exotic-looking birches, evergreens, and other trees and shrubs, giving somewhat the effect of a mature Japanese garden — all looking as if it had been there long before 1960, when I was told the building had been finished. I remarked on this. "Yes," said Griefen. "It looks that way because they didn't mind paying for it — for putting in half-grown trees, for instance, and special fertilizers. They didn't mind because they were determined to make the plant attractive."

We passed through the garden, so to speak, and entered the lobby for a brief visit. Garden and lobby were separated only by expanses of plate glass; the outdoors was brought indoors vividly. The lobby was half surrounded, too, by a

shallow interior moat whose surface was in flux — wavy
and swirly — being agitated, I was told, by an underwater
fan.

We didn't linger there, but returned to the station-wagon
and drove off, our next objective being some new research
laboratories of Sylvania Electronic Systems (where, as I
read later, things like satellite antennas are designed). The
laboratories were not visible from 128, but lay back some
distance from it, behind a knoll. We didn't stop at the
establishment, but made a slow loop around its parking-
space, which in standard 128 fashion was paved in asphalt.
The laboratories, too, were typical of 128 architecture —
a wide, low building, essentially rectangular and made of
brick, glass, and metal. It stood on low ground, fronting
a depression from which gentle mounds rose here and
there; I learned that the place had been a swamp and pig-
farm until recently. The old swamp trees were still rising
from the land — elms and others of medium size — and
yet an urbane lawn had been planted, and well established,
all in between them. This too must have been expensive,
I figured — keeping the old trees while grading, preparing,
seeding, and cultivating the land — yet again the cost had
been justified, it seemed, by the need for a "campus-type"
environment. "It is all designed to attract scientists," said
Jack Griefen as we left the place, "and also to keep them
creative once they come here."

I was to see more of this expensive landscaping later on,
but now, as we went back toward 128, Dan Wheeler began
telling me something of the road's geography. "Other
American cities," he said, "have circumferential highways
too, but Boston is unique in that hers — Route 128 — was
built in advance of the main new radials that cross it. In
other cities the radials were built first, and industry has

grown up, primarily, along *them*. The same would have
happened here under those circumstances, but as it is we
have built on the circumferential itself, which means that
the firms here can easily tap labor — and serve markets, if
they are distributors — all the way round through the
suburbs. This is a help to R & D firms because labor pools
have been left in the region by former industries. Waltham
has many precision workers, left by the Waltham Watch
Company, and Lawrence and Lowell have many workers
too. 128 runs through the Waltham limits — we are inside
them now — and Lawrence and Lowell are a short drive
to the northwest, on good radials. Modern skilled workers
usually have cars, and the plants on 128 can draw them
easily."

It was half past twelve by now, and instead of getting
back on 128 we crossed it to have lunch at a Charterhouse
Motel, a structure built and owned by Cabot, Cabot &
Forbes — we were very much in C.,C.&F. territory now,
the firm having industrial parks on each side of the highway at that point. The park to 128's east was on rising
ground, that to its west was on lower, and each contained
six or eight of the usual long, inscrutable brick buildings.

We found the motel dining-room crowded, but Jack
Griefen had reserved a table by phone that morning. "You
always have to reserve ahead," he said, "for lunch here on
weekdays. The dining-room was designed only for guests
staying in the motel, but it has turned out to be a favorite
lunch-spot for people working along the Road. For a while
after it opened, last year, you would find great lines of
customers waiting here at lunch-time. They've given that
up now — they phone first or don't come at all — but they
must phone early to get a place."

We ordered our meal — I some scrod preceded by a

bloody Mary — and while it was coming my hosts told me more about labor on 128. There was an R.C.A. factory on the Road, Jack Griefen said, that made memory cores for computers. "It makes fifty per cent of the memory cores for the whole computing industry," he said. "Each one is like a little abacus, strung with a great number of tiny electronic beads. The assemblages are very light, and are flown from here to all parts of the world. A single one may cost ten thousand dollars and be able to store what would take a man twenty years to memorize. They are assembled in this R.C.A. plant — it has an area of forty thousand square feet — by women working under expert guidance. The women need only a week or two of training, but they must have finger dexterity to start with. And that, luckily, is a characteristic of old watch-workers. Of textile-workers, too."

I asked about the transport of these women; I had gathered that 128 was strictly a motorists' affair, and I wondered how they made out with it. "Not badly," said Dan Wheeler. "Some firms who use many women were concerned when they moved here; they weren't sure that their workers could follow. But actually the women have been glad of the excuse to own cars, and many have got hold of them. There is one firm here that has a 'mother shift' of women working a few hours in the daytime, doing piece-work virtually. Most of them lived within walking distance of the firm's old plant, and when it moved to 128 we arranged non-stop bus service from that site. A survey had told us that eight hundred of the fourteen hundred women employed would need such a service. But when the time came only thirty-seven used it. The others came by car. We had laid out parking space for three hundred cars, but in the end we had to take care of eight hundred."

Lunch was served, and the scrod was good — 128 is

within safe scrod-radius of Boston. As we ate I asked about girl office-workers. I had heard that a couple of Boston insurance offices had moved out to 128, and I wondered — as insurance companies need lots of girl clerical help — how they had fared in this regard. Not badly, said Dan Wheeler again. One company had moved in right near us, within the Waltham limits. It had been worried about girl workers and had made sure it could get a supply from the output of the Waltham schools — it had even financed secretarial courses in the schools to this end. "But its efforts were unnecessary," Wheeler said, "because nearly all its Boston girls followed it here. They found they could afford cars if they made pool arrangements, and now they are enjoying the freedom the cars have given them. The supply of girls who will come out is not endless, and it's showing signs of getting exhausted. But it's done the job so far, and girls from the suburban towns will take over more and more now. Those girls, and many others out here, will have a future with 128."

We finished lunch and went back to the car, beginning our tour this time with a slow drive through the two parks in that neighborhood. The eastern park contained research-and-development plants, in the main, and the western one ran more to warehouses; Canada Dry and Crucible Steel were among its tenants. But the distinction was not sharp. "When we put up a building," Jack Griefen told me, "we design it flexible unless we are making it for one particular client. We make it serviceable as a warehouse, factory, laboratory, or office, even though these uses pay different rents and have different interior needs. If a tenant rents from us we put in partitions and plumbing to suit him, but we must be ready to tear it out and put something else in for the next man."

This interchangeability, I gathered, determines much of the architecture on 128; the tendency is to put up one-story oblong shells there, mere expressions of so much floor-space. And other determining factors (I also gathered) are the rules that Cabot, Cabot & Forbes apply to the construction in their parks. Buildings must be set back certain distances from the street, my guides explained. Parking is not allowed on the parks' interior streets — it may only be done in spaces *behind* the buildings, not even in front of them. Construction must be of brick or "better," so it won't weather unattractively. And goods or equipment may not be left around outdoors.

The results of all this were plain when we returned to 128 and got rolling. As we drove along we passed buildings, here and there, in parks not sponsored by C.,C.&F., and these were apt to be made of inferior materials — painted concrete blocks, say — whose surface was already getting streaky. Such buildings were apt to have crates lying round or an unsightly jumble of cars in front of them; they looked like fragments of a more old-fashioned industrial slum. But the great majority were in the C.,C.&F. manner — neat, comely, enigmatic, and rather dull.

Zoning by the towns is another influence on 128, I learned. The Road passes through twenty towns, which is like passing through twenty different countries where zoning is concerned. Burlington, one town on 128, puts few restrictions on industry, Dan Wheeler told me, and the plants pour in there. Another town, Lexington, allows almost no industry (though it is more receptive to pure laboratories). Some towns let plants cover half of their plots, others only a third or a quarter. These rules combine with those of the parks to shape the 128 look. The C.,C.&F. people often struggle against the local rules on behalf of their clients. Waltham's sector of 128 is zoned against livestock, partly because noisome pig-farms once existed there. But recently Wirthmore Feeds, Inc. sought to move into the sector and, as its share in R & D, keep three thousand baby chicks on hand for experimentation. Waltham was not easily persuaded that the chicks wouldn't be noisome too, but C.,C.&F. managed to convince them eventually. Now the chicks are housed, along with researchers and executives, in a handsome air-conditioned building — two stories high, of glass, metal, and pale brick — from which not a hint of their presence exudes.

We drove along past the trim factories with their big parking areas, these filled with row after row of cars. "Many of our buildings," Jack Griefen explained again, "were put up originally as warehouses and then turned into labs or factories. This has called for much enlargement of parking-spaces — not always easy — because more people work in labs and factories and hence bring more cars to them. Some R & D companies allow a whole car's space now for each employee. And Sylvania Electric Products, a tenant of ours, ran a check awhile ago and found one *more* car in its parking-space than there were people in its building. There was a good reason, it turned out — someone had flown off, on short notice, to another city, and his wife had come to pick him up in *her* car and drive him to the airport. Yet still that kind of thing is typical. We no longer put sidewalks in our new industrial parks — there is no demand for them — and at lunchtime the people in our Needham park drive — they don't walk — to the Howard Johnson's in the same park with them."

(Since that day I have heard about a firm on 128 that has a building nine hundred feet long. The parking-space runs the whole length of the building, and the firm assigned a fixed berth in it to each employee. But some employees

were given berths at the opposite end from their place of
work — so they would have to walk, say, a couple of hundred yards between car and job — and this caused a wild-
cat strike that lasted four days, until the arrangement was
changed.)

Dan Wheeler surprised me, as we drove along, by saying
that Boston is a motor-oriented city like Los Angeles. It
was the last thing I would have guessed, yet he elaborated
on the point convincingly. "Boston has never had high-
rise apartments in the core city," he said, "and it has few
first-class restaurants there. That's because people live out
in the suburbs if they can, and they use cars to get around
in them. There have always been good facilities in the
suburbs, and that fits in well with 128. More facilities —
restaurants, beauty parlors, shopping centers — are needed
on the Road, and they will come, but meanwhile people
can find those things in the nearby towns."

The Road's intersection with Massachusetts Route 2,
Wheeler continued, is the center of the 128 world; Route
2 comes from north-northwest of Boston — the direction
of Concord — and approaches the city's heart along the
Charles, passing Harvard and M.I.T. en route. "Scientists
and engineers are the main thing here," Wheeler said, "and
access to Cambridge is what they need most. They like to
run in there and confer with other scientists about questions that come up. Or some of them live in Cambridge,
of course, and commute out here. Or they teach in Cambridge, say at M.I.T., and come out on part-time consulting
jobs. In any case Route 2 — the Concord Turnpike —
makes a good alley for them. And then to the westward,
out beyond 128, Route 2 feeds into towns like Concord
and Lexington. These are quiet, leafy places with good
public schools, and scientists with young children like to

live in them. They favor them also because of their history
— Paul Revere and so on. Scientists like that individually,
and scientific firms like to set up along the Lexington sector of 128 if the zoning will let them. It makes a good
address on their letterheads. The prestige of Lexington and
Concord, as of Cambridge, is a big factor in the development here."

We were on the northern stretches of 128 by now, and
we turned off to visit a different kind of plant, a large
custom-built job without the neutral interchangeability of
the smaller ones in the parks. It belonged to the Avco Research and Advanced Development Division, which specializes in the creation, among other things, of materials
for the nose-cones of missiles. The plant, whose construction C.,C.&F. had supervised, was secluded in a pine wood
near an old dairy-farm; my guides told me that its hermit-
like quality was good for Avco's needs, but would make
the place hard to rent should it be vacated. The building
was two stories high and very spread out; I learned it was
one of the biggest research establishments in New England,
having cost eighteen million dollars and employing more
than three thousand workers. Again we didn't enter, but
merely drove round in the parking-space. The building,
made up of joined pavilions on fashionable horizontal
lines, was tomato bisque in color with silvery trim, and it
had several interior courts where tall pines were visible.
These pines (like Sylvania's elms) had been part, I learned,
of the original forest — like the elms they had been left
standing, and the building had been planned around them,
so they would give pleasant views for the inner offices. "The
plant cost twenty-two dollars a square foot," said Jack
Griefen, "which would be closer to twenty-five at current

prices. That's a high figure, and it was justified wholly by the need to recruit scientists and give them a good atmosphere for thinking."

After Avco we drove by two more big custom-made plants — each with thousands of employees — that lay near, though not on, that northern part of the Road. Like the Avco plant they were low, rambling, and briskly rectangular in their lines. One of them belonged to R.C.A., the other to a firm called MITRE, a "non-profit" company that has spun off from M.I.T. and is working on things like missile-warning systems. Such non-profit companies (others now operating in the U.S. include the RAND and Aerospace Corporations) are a main feature of the space-and-missile boom, as I have learned since that day. They are a way of getting big defense jobs done without giving questionably fat plums to private firms. The way it worked out in MITRE's case, I have learned, was about like this: M.I.T. began by developing an air-defense system, at the government's request, in its own Lincoln Laboratory, a vast research establishment in the MITRE neighborhood. (The Lincoln Lab was built in 1954, and in itself has done much to attract research firms to 128. It has also — as we shall see later — influenced other parts of the Cambridge renaissance.) After a while the air-defense job came to involve big business operations — employment of labor, purchase of components, and so on — that M.I.T. thought no longer consonant with its academic nature. So the enterprise was spun off into MITRE, a free-standing concern that makes no money itself and that subcontracts with private industry for components. MITRE's scientists keep in touch still with those in the Lincoln Lab and also with those in the U.S. Air Force laboratories at Hanscom Field, which are likewise in the neighborhood — MITRE

and the Air Force "collocate" with each other, in the lingo
of 128; the Air Force keeps some staff members in the
MITRE laboratories, that is, and vice versa. MITRE is
a good example, one hears around Cambridge, of how complex the 128 type of industry can grow when it gets into
the larger undertakings. Also of the misunderstandings
that creep in. MITRE has been criticized by the business
community because it competes against private firms —
often advantageously, as it needs to make no profits — for
both contracts and scientific personnel. And M.I.T., actually one of business's warmest friends, has been embar-
rassed by the criticism. (The first three letters of "MITRE"
are widely supposed here to stand for M.I.T., but the Institute is loath to admit this now.)

From MITRE we drove back down 128, glimpsing defense plants as they flew by. We passed scores of them, and
I have since learned that there are hundreds in the area —
several hundreds, counting the shoestring firms in the Cambridge lofts. Their biggest field is electronics, but they make
many other things too. Itek, for instance (the name stands
for Information Technology), makes advanced photo-opti-
cal systems, a job that began in the laboratories of Boston
University. Tracerlab Keleket makes things like X-ray
equipment and radioactive chemicals. Tech Weld makes
equipment for processing and transporting liquids. As for
the electronic firms, they range in size from Raytheon,
which is one of the biggest industrial employers in Massachusetts, down to tiny establishments that make one or two
small, special items, virtually by hand.

New England has a tradition of small industries, and the
tiny plants are more usual here. "I think of the typical 128
firm," a man who works in one said recently, "as a place
to which a boxcar rolls up on Monday, with raw materials,

and from which a jewel-case is carried out on Friday with the finished product in it." Or as another 128 man puts it, the typical thing made on the Road is payload for satellites — instruments, that is, to go in them — worth three thousand dollars a pound.

Not long after my 128 tour I met, in Cambridge, an official of Avco Research and Advanced Development, the outfit in the tomato-bisque hermitage, and I asked him how it had come to locate there. "We did it," he answered, "at the insistence of our leading scientists. They said we must come to this region even though we had strong inducements to go elsewhere. We had a good building of our own in Connecticut, and the Air Force was offering us another one, free, in Rochester, New York. The State of Rhode Island had made us tempting offers too. But our scientists would pay no attention to those alternatives; they held out for this area. Why? Because we needed still more scientists, and they said that coming here was the way to get them."

The official, a slight, authoritative young man, was speaking of a time in the mid-'fifties, during an alarm over the missile gap, when Avco had just landed two big government contracts; the firm's scientists and technologists, led by an engineer named Arthur Kantrowitz, had shown that Avco could solve the complex problems of a nose-cone's re-entry through the atmosphere. (Avco, or Aviation Corporation, is an old, multifarious concern, dating back to the Lindbergh era, but Avco Research and Advanced Development, its division on 128, is a child of the missile age.)

"When we got those contracts," the official went on, "we had to find a permanent location, and in the mind of Kantrowitz and others there was no question where it should be. Cambridge had special glamor for Kantrowitz, even

though he is a Cornell man. The attraction of the other
scientists here, the prospect of close relations with Harvard
and M.I.T. — all that appealed to him greatly. He came
here first, indeed, with a small research group, and settled
in Everett, just to Cambridge's northeast. Later the rest of
our organization — the bulk of it — came up to Lawrence
and moved, temporarily, into a big old factory there. Do
you know those nineteenth-century Lawrence factories? If
America has ever had 'dark satanic mills,' this was one of
them. None of us liked it at first, but after a few weeks,
strangely, it began to grow on us. Before long it seemed just
right for us, and if we had been guided by ordinary con-
siderations we might have stayed there. But certain of our
scientists wouldn't hear of this. They said that in recruiting
other scientists it wouldn't matter what they might think
of the place after a few weeks. It was their first impression
that counted — their thoughts at the moment of decision
— and at that point the factory would turn them against
us ruinously. So we stuck to our idea of building a new
plant. In some ways it would have made better sense to
move closer into Cambridge — we would have had more
immediate contact with M.I.T., for instance. But some of
our scientists, again, said we must have a university atmosphere with peace and quiet — greenery — in it. So we got
Cabot, Cabot & Forbes to build our plant where it is. It
has turned out well. Of our 3400 employees there, some
1150 have college degrees, and many of these are top-flight
scientists and engineers. They like the Cambridge area in
general — for one thing they can put roots down here in
the knowledge that other research jobs await them if we
should be cut back — and the plant appeals to them in
particular too. It has prestige, thanks to its design and
location, and that's good for morale. It has prestige not

only for the scientists either; the Air Force is impressed by it, and by its being in the Cambridge area. The place is a good thing all around."

"Just why," I asked, "is it so desperately necessary to attract scientists?"

"Because," he answered, "that's the way to get the better government contracts. Of course you can't rule out politics in the awarding of contracts — they play their part — but at the worst a contract is given for a mixture of political and technical reasons. A firm must work hard, therefore, on the technical side. On that side the pattern is to try and excel in one particular thing — say nose-cones for missiles — and with that as a starter to move into a contract for a whole complex weapon — a total system, as we call it. Suppose the government wants a new kind of re-entry vehicle. There will probably be three, four, or five companies qualified to bid on it, each planning to make parts of the system itself and to get other components elsewhere. Perhaps three of the firms will make bids, and show capabilities, that are equal in a general way. Then the government will actually have trouble in deciding — its people will be looking for excuses to decide, one way or the other — and at that point you may win if you clearly excel in some important detail. So it is worthwhile to have a big team of scientists and engineers working on a specialty. That is reason enough for coming to this area. You can attract scientists here, and perhaps support academic research in connection with them — all in the hope of achieving the one decisive thing, the distinguishing part."

Avco's strong point, its nose-cone work, had developed in the mid-'fifties, my friend went on, because its scientists had then really come to grips with the re-entry problem. "It's not just a question of heat," he said, "although that is important. The speeds and pressures of re-entry are so great that all kinds of things happen. Gases in the atmosphere, under those pressures, change their molecular composition. So do the metals in the vehicle itself. Some metals melt and turn into other substances. Our scientists discovered many of these effects, then studied them, then experimented with how to handle them, and they are still doing all that. In the course of it we have developed new *kinds* of scientists even — new specialists — like aerothermodynamicists and aerothermochemists. Our Everett laboratories, under Kantrowitz, do basic research in the behavior of gases under the new conditions, and then our laboratories out by 128 develop new materials and new shapes accordingly. We have an especially useful device in those laboratories, a shock-tube through which gases can be hurled at terrific speeds against small stationary models. That the models can be kept stationary, rather than being dashed through the atmosphere themselves, is unique and important, because they can be much better instrumented that way, and the effects on them can be studied better. We keep improving these techniques, of course, and thus we keep in the forefront of missile development. Problems come in that people just don't understand. You look into them more and more closely, and then you're practicing science. And some scientists and engineers can keep hundreds of people busy. Weight always comes into nose-cone problems, for instance, and connected with that is the purity-of-metals question. If metals are pure enough they are much stronger, for their weight. The scientist who predicted that could keep a whole factory busy, doing research and development on it."

Since meeting with the Avco official I have seen other habitués of 128, and they all agree with him about the sci-

entists' value. "If you buy up another brain-factory here,"
a 128 executive — the veteran of many mergers — has told
me, "it is the scientists, primarily, that you are buying. You
must be sure in advance that they won't feel like leaving
you." Concerning the best inducements for attracting scientists — or holding them, or raiding them from other
firms — I have found less unanimity. Some experts maintain that the campus atmosphere, with trees and squirrels,
is really the main thing. Others say it is the proximity of
other scientists — the availability of lectures, professional
societies, and so on — the "constant shower of ideas here,"
as one Cambridge scholar has put it. And still others say
the appeal is more sordid: that it is stock options, or better
pay, that brings them in. Several 128 scientists have in fact
become millionaires in recent years, and others have at
least escaped from academic poverty. I know one Cambridge lady who gets around a good deal and who recently
found herself lunching at a company restaurant on 128.
She glanced about at her fellow diners. "Why these people
look just like Harvard and M.I.T. professors," she said to
her host. "That's exactly what they are," the host answered,
"except that each of them has a child too many."

Whatever their motives, anyway, the scientists and engineers do concentrate here — there are said to be thirty-two
hundred of them now in Cambridge and its environs. Raytheon, a single firm here, employs more than two hundred
alumni of M.I.T., who keep in touch with the old school
and get ideas from it. Raytheon also hires thirty or forty
faculty members of the local universities as part-time consultants, paying up to a few hundred dollars a day. Many
other figures on the intertwining of industry with the academic world here could be cited. One of the most striking
things about the concentration is the interactions — the
cross-fertilizations — that it leads to. The scientists confer,

the laboratories collocate, and the 128 firms make components for each other. It all builds up. Some time ago, in the words of a local expert, a "critical mass" of such facilities was achieved in the Cambridge world. And when you have a critical mass — the metaphor is from atomic fission — the particles interact increasingly with no outside help. There is no rest thereafter, but a constant speed-up of the work done.

THE TRIPLE PLAY

II AFTER SURVEYING ROUTE 128 I turned back to Cambridge proper. I hoped to learn something of the universities' own involvement in the defense boom, and then to look at their global undertakings. Also to get inside the renaissance more. I had viewed 128 from the outside, as landscape — as a strange new setting for strange new academic ventures — and now I wanted a closer glimpse of the central institutions. That meant above all a glimpse of Harvard and M.I.T., the two seats of learning — prodigious rivals they seemed to be — different but complementary, contending but co-operative, interacting to make the new world center by the Charles.

I found that since I had last lived here, fourteen years ago, the two had gone far toward the goal sometimes predicted for them, of functioning together as the "University of Cambridge." That they should actually reach that goal seemed inconceivable, so different were their origins and so great their physical separation — a mile of urban drabness lies between them —yet still there had been progress *toward* it. "Our link with M.I.T. is very different now from in the 'forties," a Harvard psychologist told me one day, "because now we have opposite numbers there. In the past M.I.T. had no psychologists or other social scientists, and we saw very little of the place. But now those departments have been built up, and they have good men in them. We see those men all the time, and go back and forth and work together. Some professors, like Roman Jakobson, the authority on linguistics, have appointments in both places. We are very close now."

Many decades ago, I learned — before the turn of the century — Harvard tried more than once to absorb the Institute. The latter was small and poor then, and Harvard's president, Charles W. Eliot, saw ways of fitting it into the great organization he was building up; he knew M.I.T. well, for he had previously been its first professor of analytical chemistry and metallurgy. Even after Eliot — into the twentieth century — the idea persisted. The Institute was still located in central Boston, mainly in premises built before the Civil War, and among the inducements held out to it by Harvard was space; land was actually bought, on the right bank of the Charles — across from Harvard itself — to accommodate the hoped-for acquisition (Andrew Carnegie and Henry Lee Higginson, the Boston financier, were among those who put up money for it). But in the end the merger fell through, and in time the new land was used for the Harvard Business School, which stands there now. As for M.I.T., she struggled along on her own and then in 1916 crossed the Charles independently, to her present location, where she set up on filled land along the north bank.

Today M.I.T. and Harvard, both great institutions, are launched on unexampled prosperity. Each has a huge building program that goes in for modern design and also for high structures, up to twenty stories and more. In a few decades the two places may look much alike. But as of now their layouts, which still express their past histories and natures, are very different. Harvard has been growing up in the same area for more than three hundred and twenty-five years. Her older buildings, as a rule, are of brickwork on colonial or Federal-vintage lines, and her newer ones, which have sprouted around these, are in various styles and materials, with brick on the whole prevailing. By now there are perhaps two hundred of these Harvard buildings, spread out over something like a square mile. Their disposition can't be called a jumble, for it has strong tendencies toward alignment, but it has a certain randomness as well. It has no apparent center; parachutists dropping on Harvard, with orders to find and strike at its heart, would be baffled. Strangers of any kind, indeed, are baffled when they come to Harvard, and so are many Harvard students, even after they have been around for some time. There is no analyzing the place; one has to learn it as one learns a forest.

By contrast M.I.T., while a hundred years old, has been on its present site for less than fifty. Its basic, original architecture is in the neoclassical style, which lends itself to long orderly facades and is so used in this case. In plan M.I.T. has one central building whose main body and principal wings — all laid out in perfect straight lines and right angles — have the extent of a city block. New buildings have been added with time, but for the most part they are precisely squared up with the main one, and they often express the same theme, of orderliness, through utilitarian glass-box lines of the Skidmore Owings and Merrill type. M.I.T. buildings have names, but in most cases one needn't learn these, as at Harvard, to find one's way around. Instead there is a system of numbers, mystifying at first but soon mastered, that will guide the visitor efficiently to most any point.

In winter the Harvard community, going between classes, must don galoshes and zigzag among the mellow old buildings, whereas M.I.T. people often do everything under the same roof. M.I.T. professors, hurrying back and forth in the straight corridors, have frequent contact — "We rub shoulders," one of them has told me — whereas Harvard professors, crisscrossing in their open spaces, seem more aloof, eccentric. And so it goes in other ways. Recently I have been making appointments with Harvard and M.I.T. people, and I have found the process easier with M.I.T. — easier both to get the man's secretary on the line and to make the date itself. This is not to say that M.I.T. is more amiable than Harvard, but only that dealing with it is more like dealing with a brisk, efficient business corporation. M.I.T. *is* a business corporation, in fact. It is set up that way, with a president, a few vice-presidents, and a chairman of the board. Harvard has some elements of that structure too, but in spirit it seems less like a business firm than an Old World ecclesiastical body. "Harvard is essentially a gathering of dons," one M.I.T. man has told me.

Harvard's motto is *Veritas,* or "Truth." M.I.T.'s is *Mens et manus,* or "Mind and Hand." These words are not meaningless. Harvard makes a tremendous thing of the search for truth (and the teaching of it) as such, with the practical gains of discovery played down. M.I.T., in contrast, is all out for the practical gains, and for sharing them with the business community. It takes pride, for instance, in having helped establish the U.S. oil and canning industries in its earlier days. Until recently M.I.T.'s ideal product was not the scholar, but the American engineer with wrench in hand.

That this has changed seems mainly to be the work of Karl T. Compton, the great physicist who became M.I.T.'s president in 1930. He set about broadening the place, from its nature as an engineering school, by starting a lot of basic (truth-for-its-own-sake) scientific teaching and research. This laid the groundwork for striking achievements by M.I.T. men in the Second World War. Then the Institute was further broadened by the war itself, which involved it in all kinds of new undertakings. And afterward the process continued under Compton's successor, James R. Killian, Jr., who was president from 1949 to 1959; in Killian's regime the social sciences and humanities, especially, expanded in the curriculum.

Meanwhile Harvard had acquired another distinguished scientist, James B. Conant, as president, also in the 1930's. In time he improved the scientific side of his faculty, adding good men especially in the late 'forties; as a rule these men were broadly familiar with the U.S. scientific community, having wandered a good deal in the war years and worked on various projects, often under M.I.T. leadership. Conant also founded at Harvard — with advice sought in 1949 from a panel headed by Vannevar Bush, the M.I.T. wizard — a Division of Engineering and Applied Physics, which was a big step toward practicality.

Each place has influenced the other a lot in recent years, at all levels. M.I.T. professors are sometimes awed by Harvard's prestige and erudition; Harvard ones are impressed by the brilliance of M.I.T.'s recent innovations. Each emulates the other, here or there, and they draw together. But they cannot be the same thing.

One aspect of Cambridge as a center is the tendency of its scientists to go down to Washington, as advisers. Harvard and M.I.T. have roughly equal records in this, neither being surpassed, or even matched, by any other university. At the time of our Sputnik flap, in 1957, President Eisenhower asked Killian of M.I.T. to be his main science adviser. Later on this job was held by George Kistiakowsky, a Harvard chemist, and after him it went to another M.I.T. man, the electrical engineer Jerome Wiesner.

Not long ago I asked a Harvard professor if the different Washington administrations had had different affinities among scientists, with Eisenhower favoring M.I.T., say, and Kennedy favoring, or being favored by, Harvard. No, the professor answered, there was little or nothing to that idea. "When Killian was advising Eisenhower," he said, "he had no great reason to promote M.I.T. men in Washington. M.I.T. is swamped with public responsibility anyway; it doesn't want more. Nor, on the other hand, are Harvard scientists especially partisan about administrations. Often Harvard law professors dislike working for a Republican administration, you know, but are keen on Washington when the New Deal or New Frontier is there. Harvard economists are also partisan — if less so than the law people — but the scientists are pretty much neutral. Harvard men like Kistiakowsky, Edward Purcell, and Harvey Brooks have never been out of government advising in recent years. They go down to Washington all the time, and so do their colleagues from M.I.T. It is a natural part of their life."

"Doesn't it detract from their teaching?" I asked.

"Not so much from their teaching," said the professor, "as from their research — they give up a lot from that. But most scientists do their important research, nowadays, before the age of thirty-five, and the government rarely takes them till after that. Then the government and the universities are so involved with each other now that a scientist can't think of them as separate. He must work on whatever advances science most, and advising the government comes high on the list. The total enterprise gets ahead by it."

If only equally involved in Washington, though, M.I.T.'s scientists are much more involved than Harvard's in the defense industry. "Some Harvard men work for the R & D firms on Route 128," an official of such a firm told me last winter, "but many don't like to. They think it compromises their loyalty to pure science. M.I.T., on the other hand, has almost encouraged its faculty to go into business." A member of M.I.T.'s own administration once put it somewhat differently to me. "It's not that we encourage our professors to take jobs," he said. "But we have got a rule that a man may spend one day a week on his personal affairs. That includes outside work, of course."

The M.I.T. rule gives more leeway than most Harvard professors supposedly enjoy, but that is not the whole of it. The traditions of the two places are important, too, Harvard's being more ivory-tower, M.I.T.'s more that of an American land-grant college, with a function of serving agriculture and industry. In Cambridge the two places' partisans, though not their responsible authorities, are apt to speak cattily about these differences. Harvard's partisans may talk as if M.I.T. men spent half their time moonlighting on other jobs. And M.I.T.'s may say that Harvard men are too proud to work for the community's good. The latter view was recently expressed by the science editor of the Boston *Globe,* in a piece on the local defense industry. "Harvard participation is essential for success . . . ," he wrote. "Unfortunately, community responsibility by some of our universities has never been a strong point, though as critics they can be without peer. . . . It is true that the universities have helped New England become a techno-

logical center, but more by being than doing. Today simply being here is not enough; doing is also necessary, and
there are national as well as local incentives for such
action."

These words, properly interpreted, were an indictment
of Harvard for shirking its duty in the Cambridge leadership. Some time after reading them I asked a tycoon of the
research-and-development world here — an old man with
connections in banking, industry, and Academe — what he
thought of all the recriminations. "They can't say that Harvard does nothing for the community," he answered. "Not
when you have men like Kistiakowsky and R. B. Wood-
ward, who synthesized cortisone. Their work built plants
and keeps many people busy. How can you say they do
nothing? And as for M.I.T., they are interested in applied
things, so of course they must get out. So-and-so is an engineer there, and he must know factories. People say 'I call
up So-and-so at M.I.T. and he's never in,' and I say it is
a good thing. You hear people talk this way in the evenings,
at cocktail parties, but I don't listen. It is like two brothers.
If I had two sons, I should like one to be a pure physicist
and one a businessman. So I think it is good to have Harvard's and M.I.T.'s approaches different, if they really *are*
different." We were talking in the old man's office, and
with his hands he began marking out spaces on the edge of
his desk. "Here you have the spectrum," he said, "between
very pure and very applied. M.I.T. is at this end" — and
he gestured —, "in touch with business. And Harvard is at
this end, in touch with the clouds. I think that's good."

The R & D brains here are drawn from these two clans,
with the addition of other men who feel at home in the
Cambridge milieu. One such man is Edwin H. Land, who
withdrew from Harvard as an undergraduate, in the pre-

war era, to pursue research that led to the Polaroid Land camera. Land is now president and research director of the Polaroid Corporation, which has fine new buildings on 128 plus space in some of the Cambridge lofts. Though still close to Harvard, Land teaches at M.I.T.'s School for Advanced Study, and he also goes down to Washington as a science adviser. In Cambridge, where he lives in a house on Brattle Street, the revered old avenue winding westward from Harvard Square, he is looked on as a good example of the new-style entrepreneur. "Men like Land are technological optimists," one of his neighbors here has said. "They may think our situation is bad now, but they also think it can be saved, and saved by the use of technology — by intellectual means. They also believe that education is a continuing process; Land himself has a fine educational program for his employees. And they understand the close relationship that exists now between research and development. It's not the way it was in Edison's day. Then, with a new invention, it was harder to go from the idea to the execution; the latter would be on a much bigger scale, demanding new money, new equipment, and new talent, and it would often be surrounded by an anti-intellectual atmosphere. But development nowadays is a straight-through process, with the scientist following it all the way. This reverses the old pattern of mass production, though of course the two may still co-exist. They co-exist indeed in Polaroid, which mass-produces items for the consumer market, but does it in a spirit far different from the old Philistine one."

Financial relations with Washington have become tremendously important to Cambridge in the new era, and here again the Harvard and M.I.T. approaches differ.

Both places do government scientific work on their own premises, and both receive money from agencies like the National Science Foundation, the Atomic Energy Commission, and the armed forces. But while M.I.T. gets perhaps seventy-five per cent of her budget from the government, Harvard gets hardly more than thirty per cent, and views even this figure with concern. M.I.T. officials point out that no simple comparison can be drawn from the figures. "Harvard's percentage is diluted," one of them has explained to me, "by her commitments in fields like the humanities, where she gets no federal help. Actually her Division of Engineering and Applied Physics gets about half its budget from the government, and so do her medical schools. Our own humanities, here at the Institute, are much more overshadowed by the technical departments than Harvard's are, and so naturally our government income looks bigger in proportion. And then a great share of our government money goes not to our teaching departments, but to things like our Lincoln Lab and Instrumentation Lab, which are not really integral parts of the Institute; they are experimental plants that we merely administer on the government's behalf."

These M.I.T. laboratories — the Lincoln Lab out near Route 128 and the Instrumentation Lab on the Institute's home grounds — are vital features of the research-and-development boom here. "We have six hundred scientists and engineers in our Lincoln Lab," one M.I.T. man told me recently. "It has been the great center for developing computers, radar, and air-defense warning systems; essential features of all the U.S. warning systems now in use — of the DEW line, SAGE, and BMEWS — were worked out at Lincoln. Such things have been invaluable for national

defense, of course, and they have also had a great impact
on industry; they have fed it in all kinds of ways. Then
our Instrumentation Lab, which also has six hundred scientists and engineers, is the main center in the country
for missile guidance systems. For Polaris, Thor, and Titan.
This work too, apart from its value to defense, has attracted
industry, chiefly electronics, to the region. AC Spark Plug,
the electronics division of General Motors, came here because of it. So did Minneapolis-Honeywell. And the Lab
has helped tremendously in the growth of local firms like
Raytheon."

For all these explanations, though, it is doubted in Cambridge that Harvard would care to be in M.I.T.'s shoes.
Harvard dislikes interference from "bureaucrats," and she
is so rich that she could, if Washington policies turned
hostile, cut off her 30 per cent of government income without great disruption. But many here doubt that M.I.T.
could cut off her seventy-five per cent, even if she abandoned her big laboratories (and even though she has just
raised ninety-eight million dollars, a new record for such
things, in a hundredth-anniversary drive). Anyway the
mere existence of the big laboratories is something that
Harvard would scarcely tolerate in her own fold, because
of fear that they might wander from academic pursuits into
straight research and development for the military. A recent Harvard report has this to say about the problem:

> The availability of Federal grants for project re-
> search tends in any university to divide the responsi-
> bility of the faculty, and to weaken the influence of
> the president and the deans, in planning the content,
> emphasis, and direction of research and teaching. In-

dividual faculty members tend to be influenced less
by their colleagues or the needs of their faculty and
department as a whole than by the interests they dis-
cover can be implemented through their channels of
communication with Government agencies.

Or, as a Cambridge friend of mine has put it: "How do
you control something like the Instrumentation Lab? How
do you make it conform to your academic policies? It's not
easy, because the place has an income of its own. It gets
to be like the tail wagging the dog."

M.I.T. does "classified" research: work kept secret from
all persons who have not undergone a loyalty check. Harvard did a lot of it, too, in the Second World War, but
declines to do it now in peacetime. This is another big
difference. A university that accepts classified jobs can be
of greater immediate help to the government and the defense industry; it can, for instance, contract to design
missile-guidance systems or warning nets. On the other
hand, classification inhibits academic freedom and the
flow of knowledge. It requires that certain buildings, or
parts of buildings, be closed to the university as a whole
and that discoveries of certain types be withheld from cir-
culation. (This latter has the practical disadvantage, among
others, that if research by a graduate student is involved,
as often happens, his Ph.D. thesis may be kept from publication indefinitely.) Classification also creates an in-group
and an out-group in the line of work concerned, which
runs against the traditions of academic democracy.

In discussing government help to science, a distinction
is drawn between "contract" and "sponsored" research.
Contract research develops when the government wants a
specific thing designed — a new type of missile, say, or a

new component for a missile. Then the scientist or engineer, or the institution, contracts to do the job if possible.
Sponsored research is supported for vaguer ends: for the
general advancement of our scientific knowledge, and general training of our scientific personnel. Sponsored research
is apt to be the scientist's own brain-child, too: he wants to
explore something, and he enlists the government's aid in
doing so — funds being relatively plentiful, since the shock
of Sputnik, for such purposes.

Harvard scientists lean toward sponsored research but
still hold many patents and do many things of practical
use. To name only a couple of the more spectacular, Fred
Whipple, a Harvard astronomer, is running a worldwide
system for tracking satellites, and the Harvard physicist
Nicolaas Bloembergen has been among the leaders in developing the "maser," a relatively new sensation in the
research-and-development world — a maser designed by
Norman Ramsey, another Harvard physicist, is also functioning now, it is believed, as the most accurate clock on
earth. But still the basic patents on both the maser and its
offspring, the "laser," are held not by Harvard men, but by
Charles H. Townes, who is now Provost of M.I.T., though
he was at Columbia when he began the work. ("Maser"
stands for Microwave Amplification by Stimulated Emis-
sion of Radiation, and "laser" for Light Amplification by
ditto; both devices are electronic ones for producing strong,
far-reaching, concentrated beams of energy with many
uses, or potential uses, in varied fields like radio astronomy,
satellite communications, medicine, and metallurgy.)
M.I.T. men also, often working in teams, have done in-
comparably more innovation in things like, as noted above,
warning nets and missile-guidance systems, not to mention
electronics generally and the industrial uses of computers.

M.I.T. is often called the greatest technology school in the world. But not one of its professors, even so, has won a Nobel Prize yet, though ten Harvard men have won them or won parts of them. And comparisons like this, favoring one school or the other, could go on indefinitely. The two are a sort of *yang* and *yin,* or Mutt and Jeff, of our scientific leadership.

One spot where the two work closely together, on basic scientific research, is in the Cambridge Electron Accelerator, an important national asset, which was opened in 1962 (its cost, of twelve million dollars, having been met by the A.E.C., which plans also to pay a few million a year for its upkeep). The accelerator is run by Harvard and M.I.T. jointly, and a special two-handled spade was wielded by President Nathan Pusey of Harvard and Chancellor Julius Stratton of M.I.T. when ground was broken in 1957. It stands on Harvard's land, where there happened to be space enough for it, and its director is an M.I.T. professor, M. Stanley Livingston, who has had much experience in the building of cyclotrons and other particle accelerators.

Recently I toured the accelerator with a young friend, a graduate student in physics at Harvard. "This is the highest-energy electron accelerator in the world," he said as we walked toward it from the Harvard Yard. "Stanford is building one that will outrank it in a couple of years, but this one is six times the size of any earlier accelerator. It is a big machine in every way."

Our approach led along a quiet street flanked by brick buildings, in most of which were laboratories. The accelerator, when we reached it, was a squat, circular, massive concrete affair, partly surrounded by an earth embankment. It housed a circular tube, my friend explained, that was like a hollow doughnut two hundred and thirty-six feet in diameter. "There is a very high vacuum in the tube," he said, "and in this electrons are made to go round and round the circle. They are kicked onward repeatedly by radar impulses till they reach almost the speed of light. Meanwhile there are forty-eight big magnets, spaced along the track, whose function is to bend the electrons' path — to keep them on their proper course. And as they go round and round at their great speed, their energy increases tremendously."

"Then what?"

"Then they are drawn off and used to bombard nuclei. Try to picture the nucleus of an atom as a haystack in an enclosure where you can't reach it. You suspect that the haystack has many fascinating goodies in it, but you can't dig into it and explore. What you can do is to blaze away at it from outside with a shotgun, seeking to knock some of the goodies out where you can examine them. Well, we can't get into an atom because it is too small, but we happen to know that it's full of mysterious things called strange particles. We want to learn more about them. If we bombard the atom with fast electrons we can knock some particles out and study them further — study them either with an electronic counter or by observation in a bubble chamber, where they leave visible tracks if they pass through. X-rays, too, are an important by-product of the accelerator — they're the highest-energy X-rays ever produced — but the investigation of strange particles is the main thing."

We entered the building next to the accelerator, and first we went upstairs there to call briefly on the place's acting director, Professor J. Curry Street of Harvard; Professor Livingston was away. We found our man seated in a corner office beneath the two-handled spade, which was

mounted on the wall there. After the formalities of greet-
ing I motioned toward it and said I understood that the
accelerator was very much of a joint operation. "Yes," the
professor answered, "we run it by committee. It's not the
most efficient way, but it's necessary. Harvard and M.I.T.
have equal membership and equal voice, and we also con-
sult other scientists near by."

"Does the A.E.C. express itself much?" I asked. "Does it
set priorities for any of the experiments here?"

"Oh no," said the professor, "they leave us strictly alone.
I suppose they might some day veto the way we were running things, if they thought it was inefficient. But even
then they'd probably do it indirectly, by holding back
financial support. And they'd do it only on the advice of
other scientists, I think; it wouldn't be a bureaucratic
decision." (Ironically, some typically bureaucratic trouble
between the accelerator and the A.E.C. was revealed — by
the *Harvard Crimson,* a student daily newspaper — soon
after our visit. The A.E.C., the *Crimson* reported, had de-
manded that Harvard supply information on all foreigners
working at the accelerator. This was a shock to the Harvard
community. Then a few days later word came out that
Harvard and the A.E.C. had been quietly engaged, for
almost a year, in "bitter negotiations" over security rules
at the establishment, even though no classified work was
contemplated there. In these negotiations Harvard had
finally achieved a contract it could "live with," according
to an official quoted by the *Crimson,* but still there was no
guarantee against arguments in the future. The question of
which place will be boss in the co-operative endeavor —
Washington or Cambridge — is still apparently a moot
one.)

My student friend next asked Dr. Street — who had

once, incidentally, been his faculty adviser — about experiments now in progress at the accelerator, and the latter
mentioned a few. One was being done by a team from
Yale, and it turned out that visiting scientists are allowed
a good deal of time at the accelerator. We discussed this
matter awhile. Small visiting teams, it developed, are welcome, but big ones are not especially encouraged, partly
because of the problem of housing them in Cambridge.
"In fact we think it's a good idea," Dr. Street said, "to have
people from a few different places on experimental teams
here. It's not easy to get them working together, but it can
be done." Scheduling experiments was hard, he said, because they all competed for space on the premises, for time
in drawing off electrons from the accelerator itself, and
for equipment and other facilities. Then teams were apt
to linger after their work was done — to "camp," as the
professor put it. He was much opposed to camping.

He showed us a diagram and a model of the plant, and
after that we left him and went downstairs again. We continued downward past the first floor till we were some
fifteen feet under ground, and at that level we entered a
concrete machine-shop where eight or ten men were working at lathes, drills, and similar instruments. This space
was rectangular, but it led into a much larger curved one
that was the actual arena of experiments. This latter chamber's floor plan was shaped like a segment of a washer, its
curve dictated by its position just outside the doughnut
racetrack, from which it was insulated by a heavy concrete
wall. In scale the place was like a big garage or a plane
hangar, and in appearance it was rather like that too, for
it had what seemed, at first glance, to be a wild mass of
gear spread here and there in it. There was an overhead
crane, a truck, some fork-lifts, a number of magnets — big,

bright-painted blocks of metal — and a few banked-up assemblies of electronic counting equipment, which looked to me like extra-involved radio transmitters. Some devices in the banks — they were called oscilloscopes — had viewing screens in them like TV screens. Most of this equipment was for use in observing the ways of particles, and the rest was for making such observation gear or moving it around; the place was set up to do much of its own engineering.

We saw men working here and there amid the gear. Some wore khakis and sport shirts; and my friend — he himself had worked the summer before in a plant on 128 — said these were technicians. Others wore gray flannel trousers and blue or white shirts with neckties, and these he said were scientists, engineers, or graduate students. "Experiments here are a team proposition," he explained, "as you have gathered. That is a phenomenon of the past ten or fifteen years. Experiments are backed by the A.E.C., the Navy, the Air Force, the Army — on a smaller scale — or the National Science Foundation. Or one of the private foundations, of course." He waved toward a bank of electronic devices. "Fifty or seventy-five thousand dollars have probably gone into that experiment," he said. "It all costs more than it did in the days of lone researchers. Nowadays a team will have anywhere from three to twenty-five men on it. They may include experimental physicists, engineers, men who combine those two disciplines, and technicians — also graduate students, of course. This area has one of the biggest technician pools in the United States, you know. They move back and forth between Cambridge and 128. They live somewhere in the suburbs — their children going to the same school there, regularly, year after year — and meanwhile they themselves flow around from job to job. They are a great asset to the region. What they lack is higher education, but many of them have two-year degrees from trade-schools, and some of the older ones had specialist training in the armed forces, in the war. The better ones are a good deal like the scientists in their attitude. They crave responsibility and initiative. At the place where I worked last summer the technicians were sometimes allowed to help in writing the papers that were turned out. They loved that."

We walked around. We passed one magnet, painted bright green and as big as a small house, which my friend said weighed almost three hundred tons. "When they move it to another experiment," he added, "they can't use either wheels or the overhead crane. It's too heavy for that. They have to inch it along on hydraulic jacks." There were many other magnets in the place, of different shapes and sizes, but all massively metallic and all brightly painted, usually in green or reddish brown. They were further identified by names stenciled on them in white, among which I noted ORPHEUS, EURYDICE, JANE SEYMOUR, CATHERINE HOWARD, SCYLLA and CHARYBDIS. They looked like the names that GIs paint on planes or tanks, but more highbrow. "Magnets are used a lot in experiments here," my friend said, "because they can steer the particles. By seeing how much the latter deviate in a magnet's field you can tell something about them."

Electrons — or X-rays derived from them — were drawn off from the accelerator through vacuum-pipes, he said, and then directed against a target from whose atoms they would break loose the strange particles. Then the latter would be brought to the magnets or counters, also by vacuum-pipes. We saw some of these pipes around. We also saw a good deal of cooling equipment, too, and a few shielding walls made of big movable concrete blocks (each block had its weight stenciled on it — 8.26 tons, say, or 15.48 tons — as a check against overloading the cranes). And there were warning signals here and there, among them a revolving red light in a passageway that led around a corner into the inner curved wall. "If we went around that corner," said my friend, "we would soon be dead."

We came to an experiment that was being set up by a young Harvard physicist named Francis Pipkin, who was described to me as a "real comer." He had four graduate students working with him; my friend knew one of them; and we stopped and had a talk. The students were working at a knee-high framework, of brown metal girders, that had been made on the premises; you could see from the gleam in the bolt-holes that they were newly bored. The frame was a few feet wide, a few dozen feet long, and taper-ing in shape — its thin end was toward the accelerator, and it fanned out gradually as it went away from there. On it, the students said, they would set up a series of magnets and counters, and when all was ready, perhaps in a fortnight, they would start drawing X-rays from the accelerator and with them bombarding a target of beryllium. They hoped in this way to free small particles called π-mesons for ob-servation ("pi-mesons are the nuclear glue," my friend ex-plained in an aside; "they hold the atomic nucleus to-gether"). The students hoped, they said, to have a couple of weeks for this activity, after which they would take their assembly apart and begin preparing for yet another ex-periment.

Now, anyway, they had diagrams spread about and were working away on their frame — also, of course, becoming more familiar, day by day, with the procedures of the place. One of them explained that experimental time with the accelerator was still very scarce. "The machine is new," he said. "They are testing and adjusting it constantly, and they only run it for experiments in the evenings. But later on, when they've got the bugs out, they'll run it for experiments right around the clock, and then this place will really hum."

I suppose the atmosphere in the big M.I.T. labs, even with their classified research, must be rather like that at the accelerator. I haven't been through them and can't report on this, but I can report on a couple of other M.I.T. ventures, a space symposium held recently and a real-estate venture, called Technology Square, that show the Institute's concern for research and development in partnership with the outside world.

Tech Square — inevitably so called — is on fourteen acres of land adjacent to M.I.T., where stood a dingy old Lever Brothers plant when last I lived in Cambridge (before the Lever headquarters, that is, moved to New York). The old plant has been torn down now, along with a neighboring residential slum; and M.I.T., in combination with Cabot, Cabot & Forbes, is erecting four buildings there for commercial use and for companies and agencies that want a close link with M.I.T. personnel. The first building, up already, and nine stories high, is elegantly made of cast stone and concrete, and is occupied by some dozen organizations including IBM, the Institute of Naval Studies, and ARPA (Advanced Research Project Administration), which is a computer-research body of the Air Force. The second building is now under construction, and the third and fourth — one of which may be twenty-seven stories high — should go up in the next few years. The Square has been designed very much with a view to attracting scientists and keeping them happy. In their upper stories the buildings will have a pleasant outlook over M.I.T., the Charles, and the Boston skyline; they will have plenty of parking space; and they will, according to the C.,C.&F. brochure, be "grouped around a landscaped plaza to create a country-quiet environment." In short they will duplicate, so far as possible, the qualities that C.,C.&F. have found helpful in making 128 a good scientific habitat. They will also, of course, bring tax revenues to Cambridge — a help in M.I.T.'s town-and-gown relationship* — and will alleviate the slumminess of the Institute's environs.

The space symposium was held in November 1962, amid an atmosphere of local concern because Houston, Texas, rather than the Cambridge area, had been chosen as the main center for Project Apollo, the moon-shot enterprise. Rivalry between regions is a big thing in the research-and-development business, and it is a contest where the Cambridge world, while holding several of the high cards, does not hold them all. Cambridge-area firms and products tend to be small in scale, which means that contracts for things like air-frames are more apt to go, say, to Southern California. Then Northern California — the San Francisco Bay region — is about as attractive as Cambridge to scientists,

---

* Cambridge's town-and-gown relations are bad, but they are often said to be less so in M.I.T.'s case than in Harvard's. Apart from Tech Square, M.I.T. has a policy of contributing large sums to Cambridge in lieu of taxes. It is also especially progressive in the employment of Negroes. And its chairman, James Killian, is head of the Citizens' Advisory Committee of Cambridge, which helps try to solve municipal problems. Then, too, the Institute is surrounded by industrial areas into which it can expand with relative ease, whereas Harvard must expand into residential areas, causing evictions and bad feeling. These facts, it is sometimes argued, make M.I.T. more popular, or less unpopular, with the neighbors than Harvard. But nowhere in Cambridge is the town-and-gown relation ideal. See page 184.

which makes it a strong contender (and Stanford University, in the Bay region, has been promoting a big industrial park, a sort of built-in 128, of its own). After Cambridge and California the candidates shade off, but there are still some others. A high official of Itek, on 128, said recently that his firm could get along all right in any of five places: here, Southern California, Northern California, the neighborhood of Princeton, New Jersey, or (soon) the neighborhood of Houston itself. He didn't include the Middle West — nor do others here include it when discussing the subject — because it has the reputation of repelling scientists. The Deep South has the same reputation, at least where first-class men are concerned; such men don't like, one hears, to live in places where race is such an issue.

(The research-and-development map is subject to change, I have been told by an expert in Cabot, Cabot & Forbes, because several new regions want to get in on it. "Most metropolitan areas with any university relationship," this man says, "have been watching M.I.T. Cleveland, for one, is building a research-oriented industrial park called University Circle. The University of Connecticut also wants to start a park. People at the Universities of Pennsylvania, California, Detroit, and Chicago have asked to discuss the matter with us, and so has Dallas. It's a very widespread movement.")

Opinions in Cambridge differ as to how Houston got the Apollo job. One well-informed man here has said he believes it resulted from an unbiased, "sophisticated" decision by high national planners: to found a big settlement — "a new city of three million people will grow up there within ten years"— in a relatively empty part of the country. There are many in the Cambridge community, though, who blame politicking by Southwesterners like the late

Senator Kerr of Oklahoma, who was chairman of the
Senate Aeronautics and Space Committee until his death
in January 1963. ("Kerr used to tell our firm," a 128 man
said, "that if we built a plant in Tulsa we would be
favorably considered for space contracts. And he told
others the same thing.")

Houston got the job anyway, to the chagrin of research-
and-development firms here, nearly all of whom had stood
to gain by a decision favoring 128. After the award a great
deal of study was done, by committees of local businessmen
and M.I.T. faculty, to see how else the Cambridge world
could get in on the space program; and the symposium
was a climax of that effort. M.I.T. has a regular series of
industrial symposia, dealing with topics from food-
preservation all the way to plasma physics; and the space
symposium, officially known as the New England Regional
Space Conference, was technically part of this. But it was
magnified out of all proportion to the rest. It had as co-
sponsor the National Aeronautics and Space Administration — along with much co-operation from the Greater
Boston Chamber of Commerce — and it was put on
lavishly for two days in M.I.T.'s Kresge Auditorium, an
enjoyable building, designed by the late Eero Saarinen and
finished in 1955, that well expresses the new M.I.T. look.
In design the auditorium — a cross, essentially, between a
sphere and a triangle — shows not only technological
audacity, but also artistic style and community spirit; it is
already the main local center for gatherings of many kinds.

The guests at the symposium were welcomed by James
Killian, who without much doubt is the leading statesman
here of the new governmental-industrial-academic world;
he is no longer M.I.T.'s president, but he became its board
chairman after his service with Eisenhower. He was at the

symposium against his doctor's advice, but he carried it off well. He is a grave, mild, modest-seeming person with pouchy cheeks, gray hair slicked back, and a precise, quiet way of talking in a slightly Southern accent. Today he wore a dark-blue suit, white shirt, dark tie, and black shoes and socks. He made some remarks about a triple-play combination — mentioning Tinker to Evers to Chance and government to education to business — and then he got the Mayor of Cambridge, a giant named Ed Crane, up on the stage. Crane talked about his city as the "Times Square of American Education" and America's "Architectural Garden." He alluded to the world's biggest magnet, now being built at M.I.T. — "to guarantee our permanent attractiveness"— and he spoke appreciatively of Tech Square's contribution to the blitzing out of slums. Then he withdrew and Killian spoke some more, about what he called "New England's Common Market," namely the "symbiosis" of education and business here. He dwelt a bit on New England's strength in electronics, which is vital to the space program, and also on the way she might use that program for the advancement of science. Then before closing he tactfully paid tribute to some New Englanders — among them Purcell of Harvard, Land of Polaroid, and also Congressman John W. McCormack of Massachusetts, the House Majority Leader — who had helped get NASA launched. Killian himself had been NASA's main architect, but he seemed glad to give all the credit he could to others.

The meeting's permanent chairman was Dr. John V. Harrington, head of the Radio Physics Division in M.I.T.'s Lincoln Lab; Dr. Killian described him as the holder of several patents. He was a tallish, square-cut man with iron-gray hair in pompadour — a simple speaker with a burry accent — and like Killian he was dressed conservatively in a dark suit, white shirt, and dark tie. Indeed the whole audience — a couple of hundred assorted professors, businessmen, and government officials — were dressed in that style. The tweedy or rumpled side of academic life was hardly in evidence.

The first speaker introduced by Dr. Harrington was Dr. Lincoln Bloomfield, Associate Professor of Political Science at M.I.T., who specializes in the politics of space. He talked about the political and diplomatic sides of space exploration, also about the question of military versus civil control of our own space program (he favored the latter). He seemed a thoughtful man who knew his field. He talked about the threats to peace that might come as nations sent more and more satellites over each other's territory, and about how to cope with these. And he touched on the national-status-symbol aspect of space programs.

He was followed by Dr. Howard W. Johnson, Dean of M.I.T.'s School of Industrial Management and a specialist on the running of large enterprises, who dealt with the economics of the space program and of research and development generally — with problems like technological unemployment, that is, and the risk of inflation, and the difficulties of getting industry to invest much in basic research. He said some startling things as he went along. He predicted that we would spend fifteen or twenty billion dollars annually on the space program by 1970. Also that we would need 54,000 new scientists and engineers in fiscal 1962 and about 48,500 in fiscal 1963. "The question is," he said, "where can we find that many scientists and engineers? Let us not forget that by outbidding them from other employment we are not doing the economy any good; nor do we achieve anything by elevating a technician to the status of a scientist or engineer." Later he dwelt on the economic gains the country might expect from all this expenditure — gains in such fields as medicine, communications, and weather forecasting. "According to one [expert]," he said, "a mere 10 per cent improvement in forecasting efficiency will save us a hundred million dollars yearly. With our weather satellites such improvements are well within reach."

The next speaker, the last of the morning, was Abraham Hyatt, NASA's Director of Plans and Program Evaluation, who described his agency's goals. He illustrated his talk with charts and drawings, projected on a screen, that made me feel almost like a boy again, reading the popular-science magazines. One chart showed how NASA hoped to have a manned laboratory in orbit (after 1968), a manned landing on the moon (before 1970), a manned lunar station (after 1970), and manned stations on certain planets (after 1980). Then drawings showed some of the weird vehicles that might be used in these achievements, and finally pictures of Mars and Venus were flashed on, with captions asking questions about them. "IS THERE LIFE ON MARS?" asked the Mars caption. "IF SO, IS IT EARTHLIKE? IS THERE WATER ON MARS? WHAT IS THE ATMOS-PHERE LIKE? COULD A MAN LIVE ON MARS?" I couldn't wholly drive my imagination to take these matters seriously, but the research-and-development people around me couldn't indulge *their* imaginations that way. Not, at least, if they hoped to beat Houston.

There was a lunch that day, at which President Stratton spoke, but I had to miss it and miss the afternoon session too, where some distinguished scientists talked about outer space. The following list of topics and speakers of the afternoon, however, may give the idea: *Cosmic Rays and Space Research,* by Bruno B. Rossi, M.I.T. Professor of

Physics; *Radiometric Study of Planetary Atmospheres,* by
Alan H. Bartlett, M.I.T. Associate Professor of Electrical
Engineering; *Meteorology and Planetary Fluid Dynamics,*
by Jule G. Charnley, M.I.T. Professor of Meteorology;
The Orbiting Astronomical Observatory, by Leo Gold-
berg, Harvard Professor of Astronomy; and finally *Radar,
Communications, and Electromagnetic Waves in Space,* by
the symposium's chairman, Dr. Harrington.

That evening there was a banquet, addressed by Robert
C. Seamans, Jr., an old M.I.T. man who is NASA's Associate Administrator; and the next morning other officials
— representing the Defense Department, the National Science Foundation, the A.E.C., and NASA again — continued to brief the audience on Washington's space plans
and on the "hardware" that might be used for them.
Again speculative drawings, fantastic to me, were shown of
this hardware — the term is common in the research-and-
development game. I listened to the speakers most of the
time, but now and then I wandered out into the lobby,
where still other hardware, designed at M.I.T., was shown
in drawings, models, and actual specimens; some were
jewel-like little instruments to go in satellites.

One speaker of the morning was not an official, but
another academic scientist, Dr. James Van Allen of the
University of Iowa, who had recently discovered the Van
Allen radiation belts around the earth. He was there to
tell of an eight-week conference on space research, held at
Iowa the summer before and attended by some seventy-five
experts. Among other things, he warned his colleagues at
the symposium not to count on getting too much of their
own gear aboard our forthcoming research satellites — the
space in such vehicles would be limited, he said, and so

would the power in them; the allotment for any experiment would be small, and those concerned would have to accept this. Van Allen also touched on an interesting recommendation made at Iowa: that scientists be included among our future astronauts, especially for the Apollo moon visit. He referred in this connection to the *Beagle,* whose voyage was made so famous by Charles Darwin. Had there been no Darwin on the *Beagle,* he pointed out — had there been only sailors — the voyage might have brought back little information. He felt that someone versed in geology, for instance, should go along to the moon, if only to look around and know what the party was seeing.

Van Allen spoke mainly to the scientists; some of the officials spoke more, perhaps, to the manufacturers; but all were indoctrinating the local research-and-development world in general, on the great new possibilities. Their voices shook a little, for the auditorium's public-address was not too well adjusted, but anyway the room, which had natural wooden walls, was a pleasant place to be in. The walls were composed of narrow vertical boards in varying shades of honey-color — a refreshing touch of nature they gave, in surroundings where one thought so often of purely man-made things. The big stage was likewise of wood, and on it stood a charming, cylindrical natural wooden pulpit. The hall's overall shape, when seen from inside, was like that of a tremendous clamshell. The ceiling was of rough concrete, painted battleship gray, with graceful curves that seemed both sculptural and mathematical. From it hung sound-baffles with light-holes punched through them in many places; they cast a soft glow on everything, with spotlights brightening it here and there. And all around the scene the wooden walls, which too had graceful curves, glowed back in their warm wood-

tones. With the forest verticality of their strips they gave a
Scandinavian — a camplike — quality to the background;
it was almost like the background of a tribal meeting-place.
And a tribal meeting they enclosed that morning, in a way.
The world of Cambridge-128 was gathered to hear its
elders, and some visiting ones, expatiate on current
problems.

I went to the symposium lunch that second day. It was
held in different, but also enjoyable, surroundings — in the
banquet room of Boston's Hotel Somerset, which is a
baroque affair, well proportioned and done in cream and
gilt, with glittering chandeliers and mirrors. We were
taken there, across the Charles, in a big, well-ordered fleet
of buses; we were fed — when seated at the many sparkling
tables — a good meal centered on roast lamb; and after it
we were addressed by two Chamber of Commerce officials
and another M.I.T. professor. The Chamber of Commerce
officials, Earl P. Stevenson and Henry W. Harding, seemed
like old-fashioned golf-playing businessmen of the sort one
rarely meets in the Cambridge-128 world, though one hears
of them functioning offstage, as managers or financiers. Mr.
Stevenson said that Greater Boston ranked third, among
U.S. regions, in government support of technical programs.
Then he discussed its difficulties with NASA. He quoted
James Webb, the NASA director, as being against a
"begging" approach from the region — against being asked
"What can we do?" Instead Webb had told the Chamber,
it seemed, to produce a "new, revolutionary plan for participation by your area," and he would support it. Mr.
Harding spoke next and said that the region had over four
hundred research-and-development companies — not all on
128, but spotted everywhere like gas stations. He said the

current system of prime contracts worked against such little firms, because a prime contractor, naturally wishing to keep his own plant busy, would subcontract as little as he could. So, Mr. Harding said, the Chamber was aggressively sponsoring a space committee to bridge this gap, somehow, between big government and small industry. Harding was a tall, athletic man, and his speech was like a fight talk.

The M.I.T. professor, H. Guyford Stever, looked young for a man of stature in the academic world, but he turned out to be head of the Institute's Department of Marine Engineering and Naval Architecture (he is also a scientific adviser to the Air Force and a past president of the Institute of Aerospace Sciences). In the style of the occasion he was well dressed, in a blue suit, white shirt, and striped tie, and he showed himself a master of business-lunch discourse. He it was who had led the general committee work on space problems, and he now listed a series of projects that had been found suitable for the region — with its small industry, pre-eminence in electronics, and so on — to take a try at. He mentioned as possibilities a center for lunar development, a manned orbiting laboratory, a center for meteorological satellites, and a couple of similar things. He was an impressive, pink-faced, sandy-haired man, seemingly in his forties, and he spoke with authority and easy camaraderie. After discussing the hardships of the moon — no water, a very hot sun, and meteors landing constantly — he said it wouldn't really be too bad, for "look what the Californians did with California." He also told a joke about two Texans who were drinking and decided to go hunting bears. They borrowed a plane from one friend and flew up to another friend's camp in Alaska, but found that there were no guns in the place, only knives. So they drank some more, and then one took a knife and wandered

off outdoors. He was gone awhile, then came running back
with a bear in pursuit. Just short of the cabin he dodged
aside, and the bear itself went hurtling through the door-
way. "You skin that one," he shouted to his friend, "and
I'll go round up another."

These jokes brought laughter and a pleasant mood.

Dr. Stever left right after his talk — he was off on a
plane for Southern California — and then the remaining
guests at the long head table were introduced. They included an Air Force general, an Army colonel, and six
other men — three industrialists and three more professors
— who would take part in a panel discussion that afternoon. So we bussed back to the auditorium, where we found
a commodious V-shaped desk now on the stage, embellished
by six microphones, six tumblers of water, and six placards
with the panel members' names on them. The latter then
took their places, the industrialists on one arm of the V
and the professors on the other. The industrialists — who
didn't look at all like golf-players this time — were Dr.
Arthur Kantrowitz, Vice-President of the Avco Corporation; Dr. Martin Schilling, Vice-President of the Raytheon
Manufacturing Company; and Dr. Milton Greenberg,
President of the Geophysics Corporation of America. The
professors were Dr. Fred Whipple, the Harvard astronomer, Dr. C. Stark Draper, who is head — among other
things — of the M.I.T. Instrumentation Laboratory, and
Dr. Ross McFarland, of Harvard's School of Public Health,
who is a student of what happens to humans in space.

Some of the experts talked about their specialties, others
did not. Dr. Whipple was chairman of the panel and said
little on his own. Dr. Draper, who is one of the biggest men
in the research-and-development field, also said little; he

was a gray-haired, soft-spoken, rather jowly man, with a
nice smile and a furrowed brow. Dr. McFarland, who was
tall and dignified, put in a plea, with tongue somewhat in
cheek, for the human factor in our space plans; he touted
man as a "readily available servomechanism" and ascribed
various other machine virtues to him. Dr. Greenberg made
some points about the region and its "unique university-
industry complex." These seemed well taken, but they were
already familiar to me, and on the whole I got the most out
of Drs. Kantrowitz and Schilling.

The former was a big heavy-set man with huge black
eyebrows and a bright red tie. I knew of him, already, as
an expert on the re-entry of nose-cones into the earth's
atmosphere, but today he spoke as a social philosopher. In
its diversity, he said, the U.S. is the direct opposite of its
main competitor (meaning Russia). He quoted Thomas
Jefferson on the free marketplace of ideas. "Boston," he
continued, "has the image of an intellectually dominated
community more than any other place in our country.
. . . We should expect that here will be nurtured an independent point of view." He suggested that the region
should be going down to NASA and expressing this independent view — should be trying to lead NASA, that is,
not be led by it. And he said more in the same vein. He
seemed jovial and thoughtful and was fun to hear.

Dr. Schilling, a German-born rocket expert whom 128
had lured away from Werner von Braun, spoke in a gloomy
voice, but spoke bluntly as well and to the point. He said
this region should "think big" about electronics, for electronics needed a large array of talent drawn from different
disciplines, and that was just what the region had. Indeed,
its strength in the field was so great, he felt, that it could
"twist NASA's arm." He thought the future looked promis-

ing too, since no part of space exploration, like no part of modern warfare, was possible without electronics. The space program, he said moreover, would assume the continuous quick growth that had characterized the electronics field itself. And so on. Schilling's company, Raytheon, is among the greatest electronics firms on earth, and he spoke, however glumly in manner, as if he knew what he was talking about.

After the six members had finished, the floor was thrown open for discussion. Typically — technologically — this was conducted over two wireless mikes, looking like big silver wands, that were carried about through the audience by young men. The mikes had no visible connection with the public-address system, but the voice of anyone who spoke to them boomed out over it. Mr. Stevenson, of the Chamber, talked again about a possible regional organization, and so did James McCormack, a retired Air Force general who is now an M.I.T. vice-president. (The question of this organization was left up in the air at the meeting, but a few months later the creation was announced of a body, called Bay State Science Foundation, that will presumably co-ordinate the space effort here. And NASA has also decided meanwhile to put a fifty-million-dollar space electronics laboratory in the Boston region.)

The men on the stage joined in the general discussion. Someone remarked that the Grumman Aircraft Engineering Corporation, on Long Island, had got the contract for the Apollo mission's landing vehicle, and this prompted Dr. Schilling to say flatly that NASA had been mistaken in its choice — the agency should have come to the Boston region, he said, and availed itself of Raytheon's and Sylvania's and Avco's various competences. At these words Avco's Dr. Kantrowitz beamed all over and shook Dr. Schilling's hand.

Later on a tension developed between the Harvard and M.I.T. viewpoints. One or another of the Harvard men made some rather ivy-clad remarks — or so they may have seemed — about the "interdisciplinary scramble" and the pursuit of money by academicians. So back into the fray came Dr. Kantrowitz. "I detect a social movement," he said. "It is the university-centered community. We lead in this development here, and we do so spontaneously, without having planned it. But others have learned by our example, and *they* are planning. Stanford is doing it. So is the University of Pittsburgh. These other communities will be competitors of ours. But we are in many ways superior to them, especially if we can overcome the kind of withdrawal that characterizes certain universities — and at the same time, of course, overcome an anti-intellectualism that may exist in the public. . . . One must take a hard look at the role of universities in this community development."

And with that the meeting ended, except for a brief farewell by Chairman Harrington. "I'll see you in space," the Chairman said, using a phrase now current in these parts.

THE HARVARD GLOBALISTS

III CAMBRIDGE'S FLOWERING as a center is marked by a new cosmopolitanism, quickly apparent to the returning visitor. I sensed it now. During my stay in 1948–49 I had rarely seen Indians or Africans around Harvard Square; but now, in 1962, there was scarcely a street scene without them. It was winter when I first came back, and the Indian women looked especially exotic. They would have shawls on their heads, then extra-fuzzy wool overcoats; then — below these — the voluminous bottoms of their saris would appear, and then finally would come extravagant pedestals of wool stockings and overshoes. And the Indian men would be wrapped up correspondingly. As for the Africans, who were virtually all male, they looked exotic in every season, and still do, for as a rule they differ in appearance from the American Negroes so long familiar here, and their clothes are in native style or are apt to be cut on British lines. These outlanders are the most striking additions visually, but there are many other new foreign touches too, and the same goes for the region of M.I.T., a mile away; the Institute is swarming now with foreign students, foreign teachers, and foreign visitors of every kind.

The Harvard Square vicinity boasts at least four European coffee-shops now — two French, one Italian, and one Spanish — which I believe have come in the past few years. It also has two brand new Japanese restaurants. Fourteen years ago the Cambridge world had one or two Chinese restaurants of the Cantonese, or Chinatown, type long familiar in America, and it still has a couple of them; but meanwhile two of the more novel and authentic *Northern* Chinese places — dealing in Shanghai, Szechwan, and Peking cookery — have been added. These are farther out in the suburbs (where they can, among other things, attract a lunch trade from Route 128), but still they are quickly accessible from the Square and M.I.T., and they figure closely in the lives of Cambridge's many Chinese refugees, not to mention its many Americans with Chinese interests. Then — near the Square again — there is the Brattle Theater, which shows the best of foreign films, and *in* the Square there is a well-stocked international newsstand. There are many other things too, like the infiltration of Cambridge's grocery stores, notably the staid old Edwin R. Sage Co., with foreign foods and wines. The Cambridge eating-houses are poor — a reflection, perhaps, of incorrigible student taste — but the home cooking is both excellent and international, the local hostesses being alert, competitive, and widely traveled if not actually foreign born.

Cambridge has gained a lot from faraway upheavals. A number of Hitler refugees have settled here, in private life and in the universities — the local faculties, of both arts and sciences, are leavened throughout with men from Germany, Austria, and other parts of Europe. Then there is a smaller Chinese colony, of refugees from Communism, and a steady stream comes in from less violently chaotic lands.

Japanese arrive often. "I am always meeting Japanese businessmen," a Harvard professor said to me recently. "Why
always Japanese businessmen, I wonder." British immigrants — scientists and other scholars — come too. Quintin
Hogg, the British Secretary of State for Education and
Science, recently complained that we Americans were raiding Britain's scientific personnel. He didn't blame Cambridge or Route 128 specifically, but he might as well
have.

What draws these people to Cambridge is hard to say.
Of course there are good jobs here for the well qualified;
128 is a land of opportunity, and Harvard and M.I.T. are
top institutions, paying top salaries. Then there is the chain
reaction: the more foreigners there are in town already, the
pleasanter new foreigners can find it here. With the possible exception of New York and the San Francisco region,
Cambridge is more congenial to foreigners now than any
other place in the country; I know one young American in
town who has a French wife and who chose to live here
solely, he says, to make her happy. But the Cambridge al-
lure has something more to it, obviously, than mere job
openings and foreign companionship; the place has an in-
tangible charm akin to that reputedly exerted by trees and
squirrels on the scientists of Route 128. Physically Cambridge is not an ideal place to live in: its rents are high; it
is smoggy; its parking problems are enraging; and it has
hot, muggy summers interlarded with winters of heavy
snowfall and virtually no snow-removal — "The Lord
giveth and the Lord taketh away" is the city's motto where
snow is concerned, and this results each winter in a nearly
endless cycle of deep drifts, then slush, then glare ice till
the next snow falls; icy sidewalks, with old ladies becalmed
on them, are a winter commonplace here. Yet there is an
unexplained magnetism — coming whether from the old

buildings, the undulant brick sidewalks, or the vibrations of scholars past and present — that far outpulls these things. Whatever the magnetism's source, it is felt with great concentration here, for Cambridge life is on the village scale. You can get its full impact while walking a block or two up Brattle Street from Harvard Square, and in that space you can meet acquaintances from nearly anywhere.

The internationalization of Cambridge has coincided with an ebb, at least locally, of U.S. Philistinism or anti-intellectualism. I went to college at Yale, rather than Harvard, but I believe the atmosphere of the two places was much the same then, in the 'thirties; as I look back I feel it was almost brutally Philistine. Since then Harvard at least has changed, thanks partly to the policies of its management — I have read that President Lowell deliberately waged war on anti-intellectualism in the 'twenties and 'thirties, through measures like the Harvard House Plan. Today the arts and sciences are fashionable even among undergraduates at Harvard, and I think there has been a like change at M.I.T., though I am less familiar with the history there. Of course all our universities can select better students than they used to; the population bulge has seen to that. And the quality of American mental leadership has also changed in the past few decades, if only by the development of our twentieth-century immigrant groups — most notably, perhaps, of the Russian and Central European Jews, with their high intellectual standards. A generation ago those immigrants were toiling in the garment trade, cheered on by visions of their children's education. Now the same children are at Harvard and M.I.T., helping to make Cambridge the unique, and uniquely-arrived-at, world center that it is.

When I was here before, I had a Nieman journalistic

35915

fellowship at Harvard. There were twelve Nieman fellows that year, all Americans. Fourteen years later there were fifteen, ten Americans and five foreigners — one each from Canada, South Africa, Korea, Hong Kong, and South Vietnam. When I was here before, I spent a good deal of time on courses in foreign affairs, a field that was still organized, at Harvard, in pretty much the old-fashioned way. A Russian Research Center had just been set up, for "interdisciplinary" studies, but this was not yet prominent, and nearly all the foreign-affairs work was done within the old departments. Now, though, Harvard has three regional centers — a Far Eastern and a Middle Eastern besides the Russian — that are in full swing. It also has a general Center for International Affairs, and it has special foreign centers or programs in various of its schools — those of law, education, business, public health, and so on. And again the same kind of thing, with certain distinctions, has been happening to M.I.T., and to other universities in the neighborhood, like Brandeis and Boston University. They have all been going global in new ways.

The orbiting professor is a stock figure now in Cambridge. Sometimes he takes off for a year, sometimes for a week or two. Recently I was talking with a friend in the former category. He was about to leave on a long fact-finding tour around the world, and before going he was introducing me to some colleagues. He began telephoning their offices, but without complete success. "So-and-so is in Geneva," he said after one call. "Tomorrow he goes to Bonn, and he's not due back here till the middle of next week. It's often like that here. You try to get someone for a Wednesday seminar. He can come *this* Wednesday, you find, or two weeks from Wednesday, but on the Wednesday in between he'll be in Karachi."

And one fall, on the Thursday before Thanksgiving, I met a professor and his wife at the cocktail hour in a friend's house. The professor said he had just been getting shots and visas; he was off to Europe in the morning, it turned out, on a mission for the State Department. "But he's promised to be back on Tuesday," his wife put in, "so he'll surely be on hand to carve the turkey."

I have been looking into this globalization of the academic world here, and I find it has much in common with other changes of the past fourteen years — with the involvement of scientists, for instance, in defense and Route 128. In each case the funds for the new development have come from the outside, mainly from the government or the foundations. In each case, too, the new money has gone pre-eminently for research, as opposed to teaching, and often for *group* research. In each case there is a pervading sense of urgency — usually about our foreign relations, whether with enemies or allies. And in each case there is a factor of technology. This last is all-important, of course, in the link between scientists and arms production. But it also plays a part in the globalization, which couldn't have happened without a speed-up in our communications and which also goes in heavily for the imparting of American techniques to foreigners and foreign countries.

We Americans find ourselves amid complexities at a time when much of our wealth is centrally controlled, by the tax-free foundations and the government itself. We are using this wealth to buy out of the complexities if possible, and the academic intellectuals are one of the few groups we can turn to. So we tend to divert them from teaching, and into research or mundane operations. It is because the game is so complex that the research or operations are so often interdisciplinary. Over the decades scholarship has grown narrower and narrower, and now suddenly the demands on it are very broad. The scholars are asked to create a new missile or to cure some nation's economy, and their only hope is to get teams of specialists together. Hence the study centers and hence the big science shops in the defense plants. The scholars concerned become organization men to a degree they haven't known previously. They also get new sorts of kudos: extra money, extra importance, and the extra glamour of travel. On the walls of their studies may hang Japanese masks now, and on their desks may sit African carvings. They dress well, they are men of affairs, they talk about "when I was in the Congo." And they use special words, like "sophisticated," in describing the new wrinkles of their crafts. If you go to a lecture here by a globalist or a 128 scientist, you are sure to hear the word "sophisticated" before he is through.

Along with this globalization has gone a similar one in the Boston business world, with which so many Cambridge academics are now allied. "The whole Boston community has shifted from provincialism to internationalism," a friend here told me recently. "The place is much more open to foreign investments now — each year it grows keener, for instance, on investing in Japan. And the old Wasp — White Anglo-Saxon Protestant — leadership is giving way; one current leader in Boston finance, for instance, is a Chinese. Changes like this are a new development since the 'fifties. The electronics field is very international, you know. The Japanese again" — my friend is interested in that nation — "are good at making electronic parts. Their designers learn from us, then later develop ideas of their own and feed them back here. People in the research-and-development firms — on Route 128 and

round about — take a great interest in Japanese socio-
logical and legal problems. Awhile ago the Japan Society
of Boston got some Cambridge professors to give seminars
on these topics, and many research-and-development people
went to them. They all travel a lot too — the key 128 men
and their lawyers. They go off for very short periods. They
spend a week or two abroad and then fly back here."

One firm I have visited on Route 128, called High
Voltage Engineering, is very global in its operations. This
firm makes particle accelerators, for use in nuclear research, and is a spin-off from M.I.T. — its basic accelerator
design was worked out in the 'thirties by Professor Robert
Van de Graaff, an engineer at the Institute, with much
encouragement from Karl T. Compton, the M.I.T. president. I was taken through the plant by two British scientists; High Voltage has a British president and relies a lot
on British scientific and engineering talent. They showed
me several accelerators under construction — heavy metal
cylinders, they looked like essentially, with rounded ends.
They cost between twenty thousand and three million
dollars, I was told; one of the latter class, as big as a small
silo, was being assembled outdoors as it was too large to fit
into the building, a typical low, extensive 128 structure.

After my tour I talked with a High Voltage official, who
told me that 50 per cent of the firm's sales are now made
abroad. "Our company began in the late 'forties," he said,
"and grew prosperous in the 'fifties. Before then the universities that could afford accelerators made their own,
which was a drain on the time of their experimental physicists. But now they usually buy them from us, often with
government help in financing — sometimes a university
buys an accelerator with a National Science Foundation
grant, sometimes the A.E.C. does the buying and locates

the machine on a university's premises. Nearly all American accelerators — except the really big ones like the new machine at Cambridge — have come from us, and our output is basic to U.S. nuclear research. Our foreign sales are an extension of this. Foreign countries need accelerators too, of course — even some underdeveloped countries feel they need them, if only to lure their own scientists home again, after study in the West — and we are the great supplier in the Free World. Western Europe has one hundred of our accelerators now, Japan has eight or ten, and Israel has three or four big ones, paid for by German reparations. Others are scattered about in various countries — thirty-one countries, all told, have them. Engineers from those countries come here all the time, to see their machines assembled and to learn about them; often they stay at hotels in Cambridge, where they can find friends near by. We are also expanding into Europe ourselves, mainly because of the Common Market. We have launched a subsidiary in Amersfoort, Holland, to do business with Euratom and other European customers." Thanks to its connections, the official told me, High Voltage knows where virtually all the nuclear research in the Free World is being done now.

To return to Cambridge and its universities. When I was here before, the local academic world had one foreign-affairs body of long standing: the Fletcher School of Law and Diplomacy at Tufts University, which is four miles north of Harvard and the Charles. The school prepared students for careers in, say, our Foreign Service; it dated back to somewhere in the 1930's; and except for Georgetown University, at Washington, it was probably unique then in its function and relatively great age. Now, fourteen years later, it is still in business, but it hasn't changed much since my former stay; it continues as a vestige of an earlier, more tentative phase of U.S. globalism. Besides the Fletcher School — and Harvard's then new Russian center, which I have mentioned — there were no striking foreign establishments unless one counts the Harvard-Yenching Institute, a very special organization whose main interests were in China, particularly at Yenching University in Peking.

The new study centers have grown up not only in Cambridge, of course, but in universities throughout the country. For most of them the Ford Foundation is the big angel, though it isn't the only one; Harvard's Russian center got its start with a Carnegie grant, and has since received both Rockefeller and government money as well. But Ford is the main thing, and a few years ago the Ford Foundation, in order to allow for sustained growth, made ten-year allotments to seventeen American universities for their special foreign studies.

"When we were working it out," a Ford man told me recently, "McGeorge Bundy, then Dean of Harvard's Faculty of Arts and Sciences, came down to plead Harvard's case with us, and he did it very well; he pointed out that Harvard had just been taking a good look at her foreign commitments, and had been surprised at their extent; they had been developing, quietly and almost spontaneously, on many different lines. Harvard is the leading U.S. university in foreign studies, you see, with Columbia and the University of California, at Berkeley, close behind. Harvard differs from those other two in being selective, whereas they try to cover the globe. Harvard has no Latin American center, for one thing, and no African or South Asian center either. One special reason for the lack of an African center is that Boston University, across the Charles from Harvard, has one of its own, and if two such centers are close together they compete with each other — compete for scholars and for library and other facilities. But Harvard is also conservative about new ventures; she doesn't want to spread herself too thin. She has set up her foreign centers very soundly, in line with this, and we are glad to help with them. We are spending several million dollars on them over the ten years."

"You say that Harvard doesn't want to cover the globe," I put in, "and yet she has a Center for International Affairs. How come?"

"Oh, the international centers are different," said my friend. "There are at least five of them now — at Harvard, Columbia, Princeton, M.I.T., and Johns Hopkins — and they concentrate on U.S. policy problems, often strategic ones. If they do study a region it is apt to be Western Europe, in whole or part, as the regional centers don't deal with that. Or if they study the underdeveloped countries they do it in a general way; they pick out a few countries here and there and try to compare them. They study the overall process of development, that is, whereas the regional centers study special areas, with their special languages, geography, and so on."

Beginning with the regional centers, I have been exploring Harvard's foreign undertakings, and also those of M.I.T. and the other universities here. Yet with Harvard alone, even, the job has been a meandering one and I fear inconclusive. Harvard is amorphous at best in her structure — I have heard President Pusey, quoting someone else, call her "an assemblage of different departments held together by allegiance to a central heating plant." This is a fair description where her foreign undertakings are concerned.

Dr. Pusey himself may be aware of them all, but few others in his university are, and my method, of necessity, has been to go along from person to person, like a census-taker in a strange land, hoping to find all I am looking for, but not sure at the end that I have done so. Indeed I have come on one or two foreign undertakings by pure chance, and I assume I have missed others in the same way.

"Centers," as institutions, are not yet well defined. One Harvard professor has told me that they are mere budgeting devices — bookkeeping accounts into which money is put by the universities and foundations and from which it is drawn out in research or other grants. But centers can also be seen as more than this, as properties in which people have vested interests. There are about two dozen centers in Cambridge now, of various kinds, and each one has its staff and premises. In theory, most of the centers have been put together temporarily, to meet some passing emergency, but many of their employees look on them as permanent. They may turn out, in the view of history, to be like certain feudal properties of the Middle Ages — not like hereditary fiefs, but like the less personal holdings of churches or monasteries — granted conditionally, for a purpose, yet enduring in their own right, and administered generation after generation by a corps of initiates. In the academic community the centers are new focuses of power. They are like knots in a pine board — made from the same material as their surroundings, but different in structure. They are also like the firms on Route 128 in that they use outside resources to pursue objectives of their own. They can be seen as living organisms engaged in Darwinian struggle. They compete for foundation sustenance unless it is rationed so as to avoid this. Thus the foundations are loath to encourage an African center at Harvard, and if one does start up there it may crowd the B.U. center out. Again there is a Joint Center for Urban Studies here — linked to both Harvard and M.I.T., which is a structural weakness — because both places wanted such a center, and the foundations were against having two so close together. And I know at least one center here that is limping along now because, it believes, another center is getting foundation nourishment that rightly belongs to it.

Centers are usually headed by scholar-entrepreneurs, who can't exactly be called a new type — they have much in common with college presidents — but who at least are newly prominent. Nearly all the entrepreneurs here showed their mettle long ago in academic life; they are top men in their fields and well versed in campus politics. They can manage personnel, plan campaigns, and deal with foundations — some foundation men cannot bear the disapproval of Cambridge's more redoubtable entrepreneurs. And with their centers as tools, the entrepreneurs either create something new or at least multiply their own effectiveness, as scholars or as operators in the outside world.

The Cambridge entrepreneur whom I know best is John King Fairbank, professor of Chinese history at Harvard and head of the East Asian Research Center there. He is a senior academic now, and was that even fourteen years ago; at that time he and Professor Edwin O. Reischauer — an expert on Japan who is now the U.S. Ambassador to that country — were already giving a popular set of courses on the Far East, including a survey course for undergraduates revoltingly nicknamed "rice paddies." Fairbank, now in his middle fifties, is a globalist from earlier days. He graduated from Harvard in 1929, then went to Oxford on a Rhodes scholarship, then studied several years in Peking, which earned him his Ph.D. — more correctly called his

D. Phil., as it was conferred by Oxford. Then he came back to teach at Harvard. In 1941 he was drafted by General Donovan for government work, and he stayed in that line — serving with the OSS, OWI and USIS, most of the time in China — till 1946, when he came back to Harvard again (the war experience greatly affected his career, as it affected those of most other Cambridge globalists).

During the war and later, Fairbank was identified with the corps of American China experts — diplomats, academics, and journalists — who were destined for McCarthy-style troubles, and he himself had his share of these. In 1951 he planned a visit to Japan, but was refused permission to enter by our Army. Later he was questioned by the McCarran Committee — Louis Budenz, a former Red, had denounced him before it, and the McCarran investigators had also found his name here and there in some files of the Institute of Pacific Relations, which they had raided from a barn in Lee, Massachusetts. The questioning turned up nothing of moment, and Fairbank easily weathered the storm; he says now that he feels no resentment over it, though he thinks the general McCarthy furore set back Far Eastern studies in this country, by adding controversy to a subject that was difficult enough already. Harvard's Russian center began in 1947, and Fairbank believes the Far Eastern one should have been created by the early 'fifties, but this didn't actually happen till 1955.

Fairbank comes from South Dakota, but has long been acclimatized in Cambridge — his wife, the former Wilma Cannon, a scholar herself in the field of Chinese art, is the daughter of a Harvard professor (and one of her sisters is married to Arthur Schlesinger, Jr., a former Harvard professor and the son of a Harvard professor). Fairbank is a tall man with spectacles and a big, domed, rather baldish head, which is standard equipment in Cambridge. When lecturing he gestures a lot and makes jokes about himself in a professorial way that has overtones of Chinese humility. He will warn against the simplification of Chinese history and then add that "I must confess I have summarized Chinese history myself in twenty minutes, on occasion, when speaking to women's clubs." Regardless of mannerisms, anyway, he gives his classes brilliant expositions of such topics as the influence of Chinese traditions on Chinese Communism — he is regarded as a good expert on Communist or "contemporary" China, and as perhaps the top man in America on what is known as "modern" China: that is, China in the period from the nineteenth century to the Red takeover in 1949. Besides his talents, which are great, and his industry, which is also great, Fairbank has a paternal interest in his underlings that would grace a Chinese merchant or clique politician; his students, especially his graduate students, get loving care from him, and in return they are fiercely loyal. This gives him wide influence, a commodity much valued in Academe, because his students are in great demand as teachers themselves. "You can't get away anywhere from Fairbank's people," I was told recently by a foundation man. "You find them in spots right across the continent, not omitting the University of California, which, with Columbia, occupies our second rank in Chinese studies — Harvard itself occupies the first rank alone. Fairbank has done more than anyone else to staff the U.S. with China experts, and he is one of the very few people to whom the foundations would turn for advice in the field. He is a good scholar, a good teacher, and a good entrepreneur, a combination that is almost unique."

Even without the Japanese War, the Chinese Communist problem, or the raining down of foundation money, Fairbank would probably hold the same relative position as he holds now — he would be the country's leading supplier of China experts. But the volume of his output might be only a fraction of what it is, for Mao Tse-tung and his works have caused a boom in U.S. China studies and in foundation and government support of them. Fairbank's center plays a part in getting out the newly enlarged crop, and it also has other functions scarcely dreamt of in pre-renaissance Cambridge. It has a full-time executive officer, Dr. John Lindbeck, who spends a good part of each week dealing with foundations, learned societies, other universities, and the government. It also has a secretarial staff to help with this and with other aspects of renaissance paperwork. It is engaged, furthermore, in a contract study, for the Defense Department, of social and scientific influences on the Chinese Red army. And above all it runs a scholarly publishing program, for Fairbank has seized the opportunity to bring relays of Chinese scholars here, from the Far East, to write monographs on their specialties (in English, to help them with which language the center maintains a couple of blue-pencil girls). Thus the center is endowing our language with a windfall of books on Chinese history while at the same time making Cambridge the main Chinese intellectual center, perhaps, in the Western World. Chinese scholars come to visit the center rather than Harvard as such — or so I have been told by someone who knows them well — and while here they live a rather ghetto existence, fraternizing and eating mainly with each other (though helping support the two Northern Chinese restaurants I have mentioned). They live a rather separate life, not melting into Cambridge, but still they help to make it cosmopolitan.

Last summer I went to an annual research conference that Fairbank's center holds, which took place in a building — itself a feature of the new era — belonging to the

American Academy of Arts and Sciences; it is a big, ornate, rather barrackslike mansion, willed by a dead millionaire, set in the rolling hills of suburban Brookline, and suggesting, in its décor, the *mise en scène* of *Last Year at Marienbad*.* The place had a long dark-paneled library, with French windows, and at a long table in this sat a good thirty scholars, with pads and pencils laid before them. Two-thirds of the company, perhaps, were Americans — mainly of graduate-student vintage — and one third were Chinese, inclining to middle age. Professor Fairbank sat at the table's head and ran the meeting ably. He began with a little speech about the co-ordination of research, then called on others present to explain what they were doing. One by one they reported, and sometimes discussions sprang up — about the exploitation of the filial-piety tradition by the Chinese Reds, for instance, or about the semantic ambiguities of the Chinese language. Fairbank let the discussions run, but cut in now and then and was always clearly boss of the assemblage. His aim, it seemed, was to organize the scholars so they would give the Orient a good overall treatment in time and space, without unnecessary gaps or duplications. And as he did it he seemed (to me) like a scholarly, slow-motion Henry Luce, parceling out assignments to his staff (though not telling them what to think). He seemed in short a powerful figure, and it was the center that had made him so.

During most of my later Cambridge stay the Russian and Middle Eastern centers were housed along with the Far

---

* The Academy, incidentally, has embarked on a study of the "cultural ecology of Boston" — a topic often overlapping that of this book — in which several academic and other intellectuals of the community are taking part.

Eastern in an imitation Florentine villa near the Square
(but toward the end they moved, to a former hotel bought
up by Harvard, because the villa came down to make way
for a ten-story palace of health and administration). The
two other centers are much like the Far Eastern, but with
certain differences. Each of the three gets perhaps a hundred thousand dollars a year from the big Ford grant, and
each gets facilities from Harvard — space, books, personnel, etc. — that about match this in value, and in addition
the Middle Eastern center gets nearly a hundred thousand
more from the oil companies. The centers also do work
for the government, from time to time, though certain of
their entrepreneurs express relief, apparently genuine, that
Harvard won't let them do "classified" jobs in peacetime.
Our government security rules are humiliating — they run
directly counter to human dignity — and Harvard professors simply do not care for them. Still, a few unclassified
government jobs get done, like the one on the Chinese Red
army — or like a huge interviewing project the Russian
center undertook for the Air Force a decade ago, with
Russian refugees in Germany. The main entrepreneur of
the Russian center, at first, was Clyde Kluckhohn, an
anthropologist without special regional knowledge; the
theory was that Russia was closed to us and should be given
the same kind of social-scientific detective treatment as
Japan had received, during the Pacific War, from Ruth
Benedict in *The Chrysanthemum and the Sword.* Kluckhohn is dead now, though, and the center is enjoying its
third entrepreneur in the form of Dr. Merle Fainsod, who
is a regional expert, as is Dr. Richard Pipes, his number
two. Their conduct of affairs is more orthodox, if that
word may be applied to centers at all.* As for the Middle

* Their center has, among other things, been moving away from big team-
research jobs.

Eastern center, its boss is an Englishman, Sir Hamilton A. R. Gibb, who is perhaps the world's top Arabist and who is also known as an able executive, so able that he doesn't even have to spend much time at it.

The Center for International Affairs, sometimes called the "CIA" in conversation here, is in a brick building a few minutes' walk from the regional centers. It co-operates with them in some ventures, but on the whole sticks to its own line of research. (It runs two non-research programs also — an economic-development advisory service and an advanced training school for diplomats and other officials.) It too gets a long-term Ford grant, plus money from other foundations, plus contract fees, plus good support for its staff via specially endowed chairs in the university itself — "Clarence and Doug Dillon have been very helpful," says Robert R. Bowie, who is both head of the center and Clarence Dillon Professor of International Affairs at Harvard. Bowie is an alert, vital, white-haired man in his fifties. He has been in law practice; in the Army; in military government; on the Harvard law faculty (1946–55); and in the U.S. State Department — he was Assistant Secretary of State for Policy Planning just before he came back to Harvard in 1957. He is reputed to be one of the prime architects of America's policy to unify Europe, and he serves that ideal in Cambridge as he did in Washington. He is more of a policy man, and perhaps less of a pure scholar, than the heads of the regional centers. He is more of a doer than they, and his center is the same; it is more interested in masterminding Washington's decisions.

Two of Bowie's colleagues at the center, Thomas Schelling and Henry Kissinger, have even been called "militarists" in public print, the term being meant not in the sense of "warmonger" so much as in that of "professional military adviser," which they both indeed are — they have long been in, or in and out of, the top councils in Washington. Schelling is credited with having thought up the hot-line to Moscow, and Kissinger has certainly been one of our ranking thinkers on things military and diplomatic, though at the moment his star appears to be in the descendant, especially with the Defense Department. "One trouble," a Cambridge savant has told me, "is that Secretary McNamara has his own stable of intellectuals, and they are good. I've heard that they are much better, for instance, than James Webb's intellectuals in NASA. Then McNamara also has outfits like the RAND Corporation to help with his thinking." The truth is, of course, that high officials are at the mercy of intellectuals these days, and so the smart official will equip himself thoroughly in that regard, if only to stave off intimidation by Cambridge.

These four centers are university-wide, or at least are attached to the general Faculty of Arts and Sciences, which is Harvard's core. But there are still other centers on her periphery, in her various professional schools. The Divinity School has a center for the Study of World Religions. The Law School has a program of International Legal Studies, which might as well be called a center in the view of Professor Milton Katz, its chief. The School of Education has a Center for Studies in Education and Development. The Business School hopes soon, if a grant can be arranged, to have a Center for Multinational Business. And so on. Centers are the rage. It has gone so far that I have even found what can be called an anti-center at Harvard — a committee of Latin American studies that deliberately avoids the "center" status for fear of being isolated and made introvert by it. This may change, especially if Harvard develops more Latin American experts, but mean-

while the committee remains a loose association of men
from the different faculties, seeking informally to promote
university interest in Latin America and to shepherd Latin
American visitors through the maze here.

(It was while learning about this committee, incidentally,
that I made one of my chance discoveries in the foreign
field at Harvard. I had arranged an appointment for late
one afternoon with William Barnes, the committee's director and also Assistant Dean of the Law School, but when I
got to his office I found he had been trying to reach me, by
phone, to put me off; for he had suddenly been obliged to
give a cocktail party at that hour. I called him up at home,
and he said come along to the party and talk there. So I
went, and I found the Barnes living-room full almost to
bursting with foreign gentlemen who were too old to be
law students and who were not all Latin Americans either.
They were tax officials, it turned out, from various foreign
countries, and they were at the Law School on a year-long
training program that has been conducted over several
years now. I had a good talk with Mr. Barnes and then
ended up chatting with a Pakistani tax-gatherer, originally
a refugee from Aligarh in India, who had much to tell
about developments in Karachi since I had been there
last.)

Of all the new Harvard centers, that for the Study of
World Religions is in some ways the pleasantest. It has a
hostel of its own, set in a quiet residential quarter and
designed in brick, glass, and concrete by José Luis Sert,
Dean of Harvard's Faculty of Design — the building is on
the clean rectangular lines so prevalent now, in the post-
Mondrian era, and is also embellished, in its fabrics and
elsewhere, with quasi-Mondrian touches of bright color.
It is derisively called the "holy motel" by some of its Har-

vard faculty neighbors, but it seems actually well suited to its purpose of housing eighteen religious scholars and giving them room for study and devotions. It has eleven simple apartments for married couples and seven for single men, each with a kitchen so that dietary rules may be observed. These are in the structure's two main stories, and a penthouse above them contains a meditation chapel with whitened brick walls and sparse furniture — plain cushioned benches and a table that can be used as an altar (both Christian and Jewish services are held regularly in the room). Last year over half a dozen religions or sects were represented by scholars at the center — Buddhism (both Mahayana and Theravada), Christianity (Catholic and Protestant), Hinduism, Judaism, Mohammedanism, and the Parsee or Zoroastrian faith. Most of the scholars were attached to the Divinity School, but one was studying at Harvard's Middle Eastern center. Every week, on Wednesday evening, the scholars have an intramural discussion presided over by the center's chief, Dr. Robert Slater, an elderly Canadian Anglican priest, with a round pink face, blue eyes, and a fringe of silvery hair, who suggests the Father Brown of G. K. Chesterton. At these sessions, Dr. Slater says, all are encouraged to talk frankly about their beliefs; and personal contact among different faiths — as opposed to the more usual documentary contact — is uppermost among the center's aims. This was also the intent, says Dr. Slater, of the anonymous benefactors whose money set the place up; it is one of the few new institutions of its kind at Harvard whose main support comes from endowments rather than foundation grants.

Just about the youngest of Harvard's centers is that for Studies in Education and Development, which began only in 1962. It was founded on a grant from the Carnegie

Corporation and hopes to get added support from others, including Ford, as time goes on. Its director is Dr. Adam Curle, an Englishman who has worked in Asia and Africa. Dr. Curle says that his staff — an interdisciplinary one, drawn from economics, anthropology, statistics, education, linguistics, and psychology — is doing research on education and social change, specifically in connection with "development" (when a social scientist speaks of development, as in this case, he means the advancement of backward areas, a matter quite different from the development in "research and development" on Route 128). Dr. Curle's center has just joined the Middle Eastern center and the School of Public Health in a huge survey aimed at finding out the relationship between education and economic development in Tunisia. It is also setting up a comprehensive high school in Nigeria, using funds from the U.S. Agency for International Development, and it has started a doctoral program for Peace Corps graduates, among others, who wish to serve in more advanced overseas work. Indeed the center is in a formative period still; it seems unsure where its ideas, and its foundation support, may lead it.

Not so the International Legal Studies program, whose director, Milton Katz, a man of piercing eye, has definite views on the needs he can fulfill. His program was launched in 1954 and has already undertaken many foreign studies (aside from greatly internationalizing the Law School's own curriculum — one of its major aims — and welcoming ever more foreign students here). It has published a series of books on the tax systems of other countries. It has launched a study, from the legal viewpoint, of urban land problems (in Mexico City) — of what to do, that is, about squatters and other current city ills. And, most important, it has set out to help Latin Americans reform their legal curricula.

Professor Katz is keen about development (in the social-science meaning), and he chose Latin America because it has Western languages, and a self-consciousness expressed in literature, that make it relatively easy to investigate. ("You can't read native books about such-and-such a country," the Professor told me — mentioning a new African nation — "because there are none. Nor can you question a man from that country, because he doesn't know anything about the matter.") The Professor thinks that law is influential, and sometimes decisive, in social change — "unless we know the law," he says, "we can't possibly move in with innovations." Almost half the government posts in some Latin American countries are held by "lawyers," according to him, who have had five years — in their late teens and early twenties — of legal mixed with general education. In the view of Latin American legal educators, and of Katz himself, this is not enough, and in 1961 he toured five Latin American countries — under the sponsorship of the Committee on Higher Education in the American Republics — to study what could be done about it. With the Latin Americans he worked out a program for full-time teachers in the law schools (instead of the part-time lawyer-teachers they are using now) together with libraries, school-books, scholarships, and smaller classrooms for more intimate instruction. Then two universities — Chile and Saõ Paulo, in Brazil — agreed to the program. They, or their governments, will pay for some of the reforms if money can be raised — from the foundations, or the U.S.A.I.D. program, or the Inter-American Bank — to cover the rest. If the money isn't raised, Katz maintains, the Alliance for Progress will suffer badly for lack of trained personnel. If it *is* raised, he expects the reforms to spread through all the Latin American universities; he sees the initial two as pilot-plants.

Empire-building on this scale is not found everywhere in Harvard, yet there are other globalizers here whose dreams approach it. The Business School has its share of them, and recently I talked with a few there. The School is across the Charles from most of Harvard, and is different in its atmosphere — "the river is a mile wide here," one of its faculty told me (in literal truth its width is a hundred paces). Physically the School tries to out-Harvard the Harvard Yard — being made of brick Georgian buildings placed around quadrangles so that it actually looks like a plush New England boarding-school — but in procedure it has a crisp efficiency in keeping with the walk of life it serves. To get launched there I merely called up a Mr. John Chapman, on the staff of the *Harvard Business Review*, who doubles as a public-relations man. He promptly saw me and suggested half a dozen people I might talk with. I chose three, and in no time was having satisfactory interviews, a feat that across the Charles might have taken days of exploration.

The first man I saw was Professor Harry Hansen, main planner of the Center for Multinational Business. He was youngish, suave, and diplomatic, an easy talker. He told me about a number of foreign operations that the Business School had taken on in the past decade (aside, again, from the internationalization of courses and the welcoming of more foreign students). Within that decade, he said, members of the faculty had engaged in teaching ventures in a dozen countries of Asia, Europe, and the Western Hemisphere. Some of these had been short vacation seminars, for experienced businessmen; but others had been full-length school years; and a total of fifty Business School men had taught in them. "New demands are being made on us all the time," said Hansen. "Take the Dominican Republic. Trujillo owned 50 per cent of the industry there, so his

men held about 50 per cent of the managerial posts. When
he left, they left too. That made a big vacuum, and the
Business School has been asked to train replacements. Or
take Pakistan. The Pakistanis are developing an institute
to make economic-feasibility studies — studies to learn
whether certain industries and enterprises should be started
in their country — and they have asked us for people to
help them. That's another drain. Often we must say no to
requests because we are so involved in our current mission.
The only way out is to expand our mission and expand our
staff. We hope that a center will take care of this, and incidentally we are making appeals to American businessmen
who might find time to work with us — on leave, say, or
after an early retirement — because the need is so great for
experienced manpower. There is also the problem of com-
partmentalization. Many foreign projects are still run in a
compartmentalized way. Economists are often thought to
be the best people for development work, but actually a
task-force approach, with different talents included, can be
better. Our school has begun a ten-year project — under-
written by the Ford Foundation, the Indian National
Government, the Indian business community, and the government of Gujerat State above Bombay — to set up an All
India Institute of Management at Ahmedabad there. Now
it happens that Indian management is very autocratic; the
lower-downs don't get much chance to participate and con-
tribute ideas, a process that we in this country think so
valuable. If we are going to change that we must understand the social and psychological background. We must
have a total approach, and that's what a center can give us."

Professor Hansen talked on some more, about ways that
American and foreign business students could be brought
together, for instance, and led to understand each other.

And later he drew me a diagram of regional business-management centers that might some day be started overseas, and of how they might interact with a Harvard mother center.

The next professor I saw was General Georges Doriot, an elderly man of French birth who teaches industrial management at the Business School, who has founded a similar school, at Fontainebleau, called INSEAD — for Institut Européen d'Administration des Affaires — and who is also president of the American Research & Development Corporation, a firm I had heard of when investigating Route 128; it has supplied capital for many research-and-development companies in the Cambridge neighborhood and elsewhere. Indeed I saw Doriot at the A.R. & D. office, which is on the twenty-third floor of a Boston skyscraper. He is a thin, gray-haired, fragile-looking man, with an aquiline face and a marked French accent, and he treated me — and his office staff, whenever one of them came into the room — with great courtesy. I asked him about INSEAD and found it was a matter close to his heart.

"Six or seven years ago," he said, "I felt we must manufacture Europeans if we hoped to see Europe rebuilt. To do that we needed a factory. Europe had no graduate school of business, and I set out to start one. I went over there whenever I could and rang doorbells. I felt the school should be independent, for if a university there took it over, the teaching would be too much by lawyers and economists — too theoretical. So I got businessmen's support — from some industrialists and from the Paris Chamber of Commerce. And the Ford Foundation helped. Then I got premises at Fontainebleau from the French government; it is a good location, close to Orly airport and the Central European Command. INSEAD is *the* global graduate school of business. Students come there from twenty-seven, twenty-eight nations. Recently an international oil company wanted to hire fifteen members of one of our graduating classes, so they could be stationed in different countries, but would know each other and could work well together. That was impossible, but it will give you the idea. Our Harvard Business School should send its good students over to INSEAD every year, for a short period, to learn the European view; all the teaching there is in the frame of what goes on in Europe. INSEAD is beyond the Common Market even, for it has British students. It has no money — that's the only trouble — because European firms are not used to giving much for things like that. American firms doing business in Europe should help. The school teaches appreciation of free enterprise, you see — of what America has done, of what America *can* do. It's better than our propaganda, because it turns out sincere leaders who appreciate us."

The General seemed idealistic as he spoke. On his office walls were three separate reproductions of Michelangelo's *Creation of Man* — of the Divine finger extending the spark of life to Adam. I asked about these, and the General felt, it turned out, that they symbolized the creative function of his company, American Research & Development. He told me something about A.R. & D., which had been founded in 1946, he said, by Ralph Flanders — later the Senator from Vermont — together with Karl Compton, then M.I.T.'s president, and some farsighted Boston financiers. They had planned deliberately to steer capital into risky but desirable undertakings. Flanders had been the first president, but he had soon gone to the Senate, and Doriot, then just released from serving in the Army as a research-and-development expert, had been chosen to succeed him. I knew that A.R. & D. had a great reputation for launching risky firms and for making money on them, and I asked the General about this. He was modest, but referred again to creation. "We create," he said, "and our companies are like children to us. We don't sacrifice them if they are near death; we try to bring them back. When your child is sick, or is disappointing you, you don't sell it over the counter, do you? Nor do we. We are used to adversity, and that's why people come to us."

One company that A.R. & D. has helped to finance is High Voltage Engineering. I knew already that it had a plant in Holland, and now General Doriot told me about other foreign interests of his firms. One firm in the Boston region — Ionics Incorporated, which among other things recovers fresh water from the sea — has 90 per cent of its installations abroad, he said. Another owns 80 per cent of an English village. A third is working on preparations for the Channel tunnel. And so on through a dozen firms, besides which A.R. & D., I learned, has "a new sister company," an affiliate, at work on similar creations in Canada. The General expressed himself as wholly in favor of these foreign links — as keen on an open flow and against protectionism. Again he seemed idealistic as he talked. He seemed different from the many men with whom I had, by now, discussed 128 and globalism. Those men were far from uniform, of course, but they did have in common a certain manner, or lingo, of the academic, or military, or philanthropic bureaucracy of the 1960's. Doriot seemed old-fashioned by comparison. Yet I believe he has few equals, for influence, in the new Cambridge world.

My third Business School professor, Raymond Vernon, turned out to be small, energetic, articulate, and distinguished by the complexity of his global affiliations at Harvard. "There is a nexus between the foreign activities here," he said, "and I move about in it. I am, to begin with, Professor of International Trade and Investment at the Business School — I head the School's Area of International Business, which is the equivalent of being a department head somewhere else. Theoretically I spend half my time on that, and it pays half my salary. The other half is paid by the Center for International Affairs — the Bowie shop — where I run a fantastic operation that I'll tell you about presently. But that isn't all. I am wholly away from the campus about three months of the year, generally in Asia or Latin America. I was formerly in the State Department, and I have a book coming out soon on Mexican economics. This interest has led me to participate in the Barnes committee, which meets every two weeks, and to attend the functions and seminars they put on for visiting Latinos. Then I have close ties with the Center for International Legal Studies, run by Milton Katz, and with the Joint Center for Urban Studies. Until recently I was one of the Joint Center's directors, indeed, and this week I am booked for two lunches there. Next week I have a lunch date with Katz, to hear about his trip to Mexico and to interest him, if I can, in an interdisciplinary study of the multinational corporation. He *will* be interested, I know — that goes without saying — but still I want to talk to him about it."

"Exactly what," I asked, "is the multinational corporation?"

"The multinational corporation," he said, "looks on the world as the Rothschilds once looked on Europe. It works in all countries, and it seldom knows which one it belongs to. For instance there is the such-and-such company," he named a big U.S. manufacturer, "which also exists in Canada and which from there may sell pumps and motors to Red China. The company may go against the U.S. trading-with-the-enemy act, or the U.S. anti-trust laws, or whatever. If you discuss the matter with it you don't know who you're talking to — an American or Canadian or what. You should really ask the company psychiatrist. All in all, I think, the phenomenon is ripe for a study."

I nodded thankfully, and Dr. Vernon went on to explain the "fantastic operation" that he runs at the Center for International Affairs.

"It's a development advisory service," he said, "that has a staff of twenty-two people in foreign countries. Development isn't really understood by social scientists, and so the Center, by offering advisers to serve with developing countries, is exposing itself to the process. Some of the advisers are rotated back periodically to Harvard, where they do research or teaching, or both, to spread their knowledge and explore the subject further. We are trying to develop a third class of career here, you see — a class of people whose work is neither academic nor administrative primarily — people who are operators to a large degree. The old assumption, of only two kinds of career on a campus, is fast disappearing."

The advisory service has thirteen workers now in Pakistan, the professor told me — inherited from a Harvard planning group that has been there for a decade — and it has sent three others to Argentina, three to Colombia, and two to Indonesia. The full staff of twenty-two field people costs over a million annually, at fifty thousand dollars per man-year. The Ford Foundation is the chief angel, but it is sharing the cost of Pakistan with the U.S.A.I.D. program. And the Argentine venture is paid for wholly by the Inter-American Bank.

OTHER CAMBRIDGE GLOBALISTS

IV M.I.T.'s NATURE as a technical school, dealing in "applied" knowledge, shows up in her Center for International Studies. The foreign-study centers at Harvard get much support from their university, but the center at M.I.T. comes close, by virtue of foundation grants and government contracts, to paying its own way. Toward that end it does classified research, and this alone gives its premises a special atmosphere. Entry to the Harvard centers is free as the wind — one may drift in and out of them at will — but much of M.I.T.'s center is in a railed-off limbo like those in our embassies and foreign military installations. The visitor must stop there, state his business, and wait till the man he is to see, or that man's secretary, comes to escort him farther. Then after his talk, which in itself may differ little from one with a Harvard savant, he must be escorted out again, departing under the eye of a security guard.

In its research the center also puts more stress than do Harvard's on technological means and technological interests. Harvard's social scientists try hard to justify the "sci-

ence" label, but where political science is concerned they
are not radical about it. In their teaching, the Harvard
political scientists still emphasize the reading of constitu-
tions and of writers like Plato and John Stuart Mill. But
their colleagues at M.I.T. incline more to a "behavioral"
study of modern trends — contemporary change, for instance — with the help of polling, statistical analysis, and
electronic computers. Mathematics is a prerequisite for
graduate study in political science at the Institute (and
probably nowhere else in the world). The idea is strong
there that science is about to enter politics and bring on
a new dawn. James R. Killian, Jr., M.I.T.'s chairman of
the board, has written:

> . . . The interface between science and political sci-
> ence is an area worthy of careful attention. . . . It is
> here that the most effective bridges between science
> and the social sciences can be built. . . . It has been
> remarked that disciplines other than science and engi-
> neering may well begin to develop a dynamic quality,
> a rapidity of change, not unlike science. Political sci-
> ence may be such a field. It has also been frequently
> remarked that the United States has not produced a
> great political philosopher, certainly not since the
> Founding Fathers. Perhaps the interplay between
> science and politics may provide a new stimulus, as
> it did in a different way to Locke and Hobbes, for a
> new creative surge in this field.

M.I.T.'s international center shares in this expectancy
about the union of science and politics, besides which it
naturally dwells on topics of interest to a technical school.
It has made a study of Soviet research and development in
the arms industry, which corresponds to the industry on

Route 128 that the Institute is so involved with. It also studies the development of backward areas, where our ability to transfer technology is thought to be the key issue. And it does much work on "communications," a word that in M.I.T., more even than elsewhere perhaps, covers everything now from the stringing of telephone wires to the art of persuasion.

M.I.T.'s branching out into social studies is a recent occurrence, and it has been sped by the individual, subjective interests of leading men there — not just of Killian and Julius Stratton, the M.I.T. president, but also of scientists and engineers like Jerrold R. Zacharias and Jerome Wiesner, who have found politics an engrossing field. The Center for International Studies began in the first place because Wiesner took a broad view of a communications problem; he had been asked, as an electrical engineer, to stop the jamming of American broadcasts to Russia, and he insisted on first learning more about the broadcasts' contents and potential audiences. The center was put together to help supply that knowledge, and since then it has been enthusiastically patronized, in other lines, by various M.I.T. scientific wizards — they get along well with its chief, Max Millikan, a quiet, logical man who is an economist but also a son of the late Robert A. Millikan, the great physicist and president of Caltech.

"From the beginning we felt the pressure of the scientific community," Professor Millikan has explained. "Some scientists got absorbed, for one thing, in applied weapons problems. They had been designing nuclear explosives and supersonic planes — things like that — and dissatisfaction with the results was working in them. It burst out in a great interest in disarmament and arms control, notably among Wiesner, Zacharias, and their Harvard colleagues

Ed Purcell and Paul Doty. All those men had been involved earlier in arms development. They were strongly concerned about the results, but they did not share the old simple revulsion against war — the feeling that had moved the atomic scientists in the 'forties. They wanted, rather, to study the how of war, and what to do about it. So five years ago Wiesner and Zacharias started a small seminar on the subject. They took in Bowie and Kissinger from Harvard as well as Walt Rostow, of our center here, and myself. We met casually at first on Sunday mornings, then we decided to formalize it and got a small Rockefeller grant. Now the seminar meets one evening a month and has thirty-five people in it, from both Harvard and here and from many different disciplines."

Almost simultaneously with this interest in arms control, an urge grew up among the scientists to help advance the backward areas. "Until recently M.I.T. did very little overseas," a dean at the Institute has told me. "In the middle 'fifties we had a contract with the Economic Co-operation Administration — now the A.I.D. — to work with the University of Rangoon, but nothing came of this. In those days the problems of underdeveloped countries were of interest to few people here outside the Center for International Studies. The scientists and engineers didn't care much; they were busy with the new technology in America and all its opportunities. But as the 'fifties wore on they began changing. One year one engineer would drop in on Max Millikan and ask what could be done about development; the next year two would drop in; and so on. In a few years there came to be a great deal of feeling, all through the Institute, about these problems, and that is behind the overseas work we are doing now."

M.I.T.'s global development has been different from

Harvard's in that it began almost from scratch. Harvard's globalism has increased tremendously since the early 'fifties, and much enthusiasm has gone into it, but the movement has been led by a corps of professionals, of men who decided in the 'thirties, or even the 'twenties, that they would be internationalists, and who systematically trained for it. M.I.T., on the other hand, has had to convert amateurs or import professionals from elsewhere. Millikan and his noted colleague, Walt W. Rostow, came to M.I.T. only in the late 'forties, and most of their associates joined them in the 'fifties — Paul Rosenstein-Rodan, a famous economist now reputed very influential in the center, came only in 1953. And the M.I.T. library has yet to catch up with the center's activities; the latter is still dependent on the Widener Library at Harvard, from which it borrows in a wholesale way.

Much of the center's work on development has stemmed from the interests of Rostow (who is on leave now and serving as Chairman of the State Department's Policy Planning Council, a job corresponding to that once held, under Eisenhower and Dulles, by Robert Bowie of Harvard's international center). Rostow, in the words of a colleague here, has a "Toynbeean or Spenglerian" liking for generalization, which he has indulged at the center by exploring, and getting others to explore, the progress of different underdeveloped countries and then comparing them. Among the fruits of this work has been a Rostow book, published in 1960, called *The Stages of Economic Growth: A Non-Communist Manifesto*, which has been widely publicized as a refutation of Marx. In it Rostow, like Marx, lays down a fixed scheme of evolution for all countries, though the scheme itself is non-Marxian: Rostow has each country undergoing five stages — not necessarily with violence — in the adoption of modern technology, these beginning with a "traditional," primitive ("pre-Newtonian") stage and ending in an "age of high mass consumption." The book has had a mixed reception. Rostow (again like Marx) is an economic historian with little first-hand experience of regions outside the Western World. His predictions about Africa and Asia (also like Marx's) are made from afar and are speculative in that the supposed evolution has not yet progressed much in those continents. The predictions are not hailed enthusiastically by all students of Asian and African affairs. On the other hand they have given hope to some Afro-Asian leaders and are effective propaganda in that they call attention to the Marxian fallacies. Thus his book may be counted a good example of "applied" scholarship, or scholarship toward an end. It is also, regardless of its defects, a contribution to the literature of change as such. M.I.T.'s center has made other contributions to that literature. Leading members of its staff — such as the journalist Harold Isaacs, the economist Everett Hagen, and the Asian specialist Lucian Pye — have written largely on change in the past few years. Experts at the center have even programmed a computer to simulate "an economy in the early stages of development" and have then watched it tick off changes in response to economic measures — also simulated, of course — that they have fed into it.

Another feature of the M.I.T. center is its emphasis on the present. "We are interested in the contemporary world," Professor Millikan explains. "We have studied India a good deal, but that doesn't mean we have gone much into Sanskrit or Indian religions. What we *have* needed is social scientists of many kinds." Here again the M.I.T. bent differs somewhat from Harvard's. Harvard's

East Asian center has published several works on nineteenth-century China and at least one on eleventh-century developments under the Sung Dynasty. M.I.T. doesn't do that kind of thing.

Then the question of applied technology comes in. This can be concrete and specific at times; one company that invented a new pump came and asked M.I.T. whether it would be popular in Indian villages. The center is a natural for "techno-economic" inquiries like this; it has also been making studies of foundry techniques and village power plants that might suit Indian conditions.

M.I.T. had a good precedent in starting the center because it had already launched interdisciplinary *science* centers. "The interdisciplinary approach," Max Millikan has said, "grew out of the Research Laboratory of Electronics here, whose predecessor — our Radiation Laboratory — began with radar during the war and then moved into communications. Our Center for Communications Sciences arose from that. Then came other centers, focused around problems rather than disciplines — a Center for Materials Sciences and Engineering, a Center for Space Research, a Center for Earth Sciences, a Center for Life Sciences — each drawing on several disciplines and all trying to redefine the boundaries of learning. These things began at M.I.T. because of our 'applied' bent — our interest in problems as distinct from disciplines of the old kind."

The Center's work on Soviet research and development is done by Alexander Korol, a White Russian who was a businessman, not a professional scholar, in the years before he joined M.I.T. I had lunch with him one day at the Institute's Faculty Club, which is on the sixth floor of its Alfred P. Sloan Building (the club resembles a businessmen's lunch club much more than it does the Harvard Faculty Club, a gabled brick-and-ivy structure just outside the Yard). Mr. Korol was a tall, strong-looking, gray-haired man — enthusiastic, charming, and wrapped up in his subject — and I found myself learning more about *it* than about his methods. By the time I saw him I had become interested in the relationship of U.S. intellectuals to arms production, and I was glad to hear about their Russian counterparts.

The Russian R & D industry, Mr. Korol said, is in flux now as it is undergoing reorganization. It is being centralized again after an attempt at decentralization in 1957, when research was theoretically parceled out among a hundred-odd regional offices. This didn't work because the stronger central ministries hung onto their research despite it, and because few scientists or engineers were induced to leave Moscow and Leningrad for the sticks. The government changed its tack, therefore, and in 1961 and 1962 announced *re*centralization measures. It is still too early to tell about their success, Mr. Korol said, but he predicted certain problems that would arise. There would be difficulty in horizontal communication between plants at the lowest or regional level — one plant would need parts made by another a few miles away, but could not get them without tedious application via Moscow. And then the central supervision of regional plants would be weak, and the latter would exploit this by cutting corners — by making things out of inferior materials, say, or by making them too heavy. "Weight is one criterion for a production quota," said Mr. Korol, "and some managers try by making heavier objects to cover up for making fewer of them. *Krokodil*, the Russian satirical magazine, had a cartoon recently of some men loading a gigantic screw onto a truck — it took up the whole cargo space — and remarking that their year's quota was now filled. But abuses like that rarely happen in the vital defense industries. These are like capitalist monopolies; they can get whatever they need regardless of cost."

I asked further about the reluctance of Russian technologists to leave Moscow and Leningrad — it seemed so like the tendency of American ones to cluster around Cambridge — and Mr. Korol said it was a real problem. "More than half of Russia's 'scientific workers' are in Moscow and Leningrad," he told me. "Before 1957 Leningrad had three hundred and seventy-five R & D organizations, and only forty-two of them went away in the supposed decentralization. The concentration seems impossible to stop, but the authorities are trying. For some time now the enrolment in Moscow and Leningrad schools has been frozen. No new research institutions are allowed in those cities, either, without explicit top-level approval."

Mr. Korol explained that "scientific worker" is the Soviet term for a graduate of higher education who is in scientific research or teaching. "Russia's employment figures are more exact than ours," he said, "and we can tell something about these scientific workers. Far more women serve in R & D there, for one thing. Three hundred and twenty thousand of Russia's engineers are women — 29 per cent of the total. Women are few among the top physicists and mathematicians, but among 'supervisors and specialists in research,' a lower category, they make up 52 per cent. Jewish scientific workers are another important element, and the census figures bring this out. The Russian national average is a hundred and forty-eight scientific workers for each hundred thousand of population, but among Jews the figure is one thousand three hundred and fifty-one per hundred thousand — almost ten times as great."

Premier Khrushchev, Mr. Korol believed, is temperamentally anti-intellectual — rather like Charles Wilson, our former Defense Secretary — but tolerates intellectuals, also like Wilson, because he has to. "Actually Russia's scientists are treated much better, relatively speaking, than ours," Korol said. "A scientist there earns sixteen times as much as a common laborer, while the figure here is only two and a half times. But in absolute terms our scientists are better off. I remember how amazed a Russian scientist was — a visitor here — when he came to call on me at home. I live in a modest prefabricated house near the border of West Cambridge. The visitor was an important man at home — he had a chauffeur day and night — but he had only three rooms for himself and his family. In my family we are just two, and we had more than that, and he thought it was wonderful."

If greater freedom is achieved in Russia, Mr. Korol thought, the climate for long-term research may become better there than here. This judgment he related to the pragmatic American liking for applied rather than basic science, to which he nevertheless granted some advantages. "We are more prone than the Russians to modernization and innovation in our plant," he said, "and that is a help. We are better at getting the results of basic research into applied science. This is a great problem for the Russians — the translating or diffusing of laboratory findings to the factories. They call the process *vnedreniye,* and they are far from mastering it. One of their troubles is a division between research and teaching. Most 'scientific workers' do one or the other, not both. For a long time the universities were training engineers especially, and they did little cultivation of basic science. They got into a habit of ultra-specialization, which they are now trying to change. Awhile ago there was an article in the *Herald of Higher Schools,* a Russian education journal, that referred enviously to scientific researchers here at M.I.T. The article was by a professor, who was also a section head in a ministry, and it urged that Russian universities sponsor more research in the M.I.T. manner." Russia has no close equivalent, I gathered, to the academic-industrial partnership one gets here, between Cambridge and Route 128.

Mr. Korol's researches are being supported by the National Science Foundation — in the past they were carried, at least in part, by a Carnegie grant to the M.I.T. center as a whole. In 1957 he published a book called *Soviet Education for Science and Technology;* it came out just before Sputnik and got wide notice. In writing it he was helped by others on the M.I.T. faculty. Several of them read and criticized sections of his manuscript, and some made evaluations for him of Russian textbooks, especially in physics and mechanical engineering, which he had chosen as representative fields. His book also compared Russian curricula — in mechanical engineering, physics, and mathematics — with the corresponding M.I.T. ones. The work gained from its M.I.T. background, and the M.I.T. faculty broadened its knowledge by having Mr. Korol in its midst. Similar gains are presumably being made now with his R & D studies.

Another man I have seen at the M.I.T. center is Dr. Lincoln Bloomfield, a specialist in arms control, space diplomacy, and the United Nations. (I had heard him talk a couple of times* and was interested in what he said, and

* See page 52.

I singled him out for that reason, much as I had singled
out Mr. Korol through my interest in R & D.) Professor
Bloomfield is an alert, articulate young man and a tena-
cious middle-of-the-roader in the arms-control field — "I
am called a peacemonger by the warmongers," he says, "and
a warmonger by the peacemongers." In the middle 'fifties
he was working in the State Department, as a special assistant to the Assistant Secretary of State for International
Organization Affairs, but resigned that job in order to join
the staff at M.I.T. One of his first tasks was an overall
review of American policy in the U.N. — a job that he
had never really had time to do in Washington — and his
survey was adopted as a guide by the government. Alto-
gether, he says, his transfer to Cambridge, and to the status
of a contract worker instead of a salaried one, gave him
more influence in Washington, and this is characteristic
of the new relationship between Academe and the officialdom. Often now the same man will have more face in the
government if he sits by the Charles instead of the Potomac.

My curiosity about Bloomfield had been aroused by his
saying that three times within the past year he had "put on
games for the U.S. government." I had vaguely connected
this with the "theory of games," which I had heard of as
an intellectual element in our policy-making, but when I
saw Bloomfield he told me I was confusing two different
things. The theory of games is a mathematical activity,
developed in the 1940's, that seeks to put certain types of
conflict — such as games, commercial bargaining, and military rivalry — into formulas that can be explored and
manipulated in an abstract way. It is popular with some
advisers to our government and is carried on to a certain extent in Cambridge — by, among others, Professor
Thomas Schelling of Harvard — but it differs from games

playing of the Bloomfield sort. This too is increasingly popular as a guide to policy, and it is carried on in various universities, in the government itself, and in some governmental spin-offs like the RAND Corporation. It resembles our traditional war games, and it consists of putting hypothetical diplomatic problems before opposing groups of experts, who then fight them out, according to agreed rules, in hopes of finding what might happen in the real world under like conditions. Professor Bloomfield puts his games on for the Institute for Defense Analyses, a non-profit organization linked with the Defense Department, which pays M.I.T. under a contract. His latest series has dealt with problems arising in four projected phases of disarmament, and he regards them as an aid in a more full-time study he is making of arms control, also under contract. He has staged the games at Endicott House — a baronial mansion at Dedham, Mass., that has come into M.I.T.'s possession — and in each one he has used a couple of dozen experts — from the universities, the State Department, and the armed services — these divided into teams representing the U.S., Russia, the U.N., and other groups.

"You can't find a disarmed world," Bloomfield told me after one of these games, "but last week we created such a world for three days. We made it very real too; you have to make it real if you invite senior officers from the Pentagon and want them to play. You have to be right with your tables of organization, and order of battle, and your figuring out of airlift and sealift. It was very complicated this time. Our problem was in 1972, and we assumed an international police force of fifteen thousand men stationed in Bizerte." He went on to tell how he had worked out the movement of the force with experts in the Defense Department — the problem concerned a crisis in Latin America — and how he had got a young professor at Yale to write a 'scenario' for it (of some fifty pages, which was then duplicated, for the players, into dozens of purple-ink copies).

"I sometimes write the scenario myself," he said. "It's hard to persuade the military, you know, that disarmament will ever be a reality. You have to make it plausible; you have to tell them, for instance, that some weapons went off by mistake and frightened the powers into arms control. Then you tell them what kind of world exists at the time of the problem — what the conditions are economically and technologically. Then they are turned loose and must make their moves as Russians, Americans, or whatever. They learn things in a way they have never learned them before. One of the interesting things is to take Russian experts and make them live with their predictions; I have known such experts to be surprised when they see, for instance, how much the strategic interests of Russia and China hold together in a crisis. Games are a good way of teaching, as well as of finding things out by experiment. And also of bringing out minority opinions. There is a pressure for conformity around an ordinary conference table, but this doesn't exist at a game."

I asked Dr. Bloomfield if his games weren't rather abstract, and he told me they were too *concrete* in the opinion of some experts — of the gaming authorities, for instance, at one university he named, where they confine themselves to dealing with concepts like "Country A" and "Country B" instead of real nations. He told me more about his games too, but they are really a minor activity of his, and it would be wrong to dwell on them too much. His main work is the study of arms control in a more conventional way, though while pursuing it (and teaching two or three courses) he also keeps up with U.N. affairs and with space politics. His arms-control research was launched with a twenty-five-thousand-dollar grant from the Rockefeller Foundation. Its aim was to study arms control in relation to our foreign policy, especially in view of the development of international police forces. As an aid in this Bloomfield visited the Gaza Strip and the Congo, where such forces were in use, in 1962. Since then the tab for his work has been picked up by the Arms Control and Disarmament Agency, which has negotiated two contracts with M.I.T. One, whose fee is sixty-five thousand dollars, calls for a study of the Soviet Union and arms control. The other, whose fee is one hundred and forty-five thousand, calls for a study of *regional* arms control and the developing countries — of how our diplomatic problems in Asia, Africa, and Latin America may alter with changes in the global arms set-up. Dr. Bloomfield has subcontracted certain parts of this latter study to the Harvard Middle Eastern and B.U. African centers and the Columbia University Institute of War and Peace Studies. Meanwhile he has enlarged his own staff at the center in M.I.T. and is a very busy man—his arms-control games for I.D.A. (fee forty-five thousand) are now finished, but he is running another series of games, on nuclear deterrence, for the Navy.

M.I.T.'s standing as a fine technology school — the finest, without much doubt, in the world — has led it into several foreign ventures. NATO is considering the creation of a European M.I.T., directly patterned on the Institute, and Chairman Killian, along with some of his professors, is helping personally in the deliberations. Then an Indian Institute of Technology has already been started. The Indian government asked M.I.T. to be the sole foreign adviser on the project, but the Institute declined through fear of spreading its resources too thin. It got up a consortium of nine American universities to do the job together. The co-ordination was put in the hands of Educational Services Incorporated, an M.I.T. spin-off created originally for other purposes.* M.I.T.'s preliminary study for the I.I.T. was paid for by the Ford Foundation, but the angel now is the U.S.A.I.D. administration. A.I.D. has also set up a second E.S.I. consortium to do an educational job at Kabul in Afghanistan. And the M.I.T. Sloan School of Management is building up a business school in Calcutta — directly, without E.S.I. intervention — that will be comparable to the Harvard business school at Ahmedabad. There are lesser foreign offshoots too, and in general M.I.T.'s influence, like Harvard's, is becoming global very fast.

The global currents flowing back to M.I.T. are so like Harvard's that we needn't dwell on them. The Institute's proportion of foreign students — 12 per cent — is the second highest in America (the first being that at Howard University, in Washington). The place also has a program, "M.I.T. Fellows in Africa," that puts U.S. students holding graduate degrees into functional African jobs — mainly government ones — for two-year terms. It has another program whereby M.I.T. undergraduate civil engineers do summer work in Latin America. And so on.

With the rest of Cambridge's academic world it is much the same. The Fletcher School at Tufts is still going strong. Brandeis University, though a newcomer, is getting well launched in foreign affairs. She already has a program, financed by Lawrence A. Wien, a New York philanthropist,

* See pp. 163ff.

that supports some sixty-five foreign students on her campus every year. She is sending some thirty American students — juniors — to Israel each year for six months of study (including eight weeks in an *ulpan,* or intensive Hebrew-language course). She is also working up a close relationship with at least one Latin American University, the University of the Andes at Bogotá. And in two recent summers she has run a seminar on America for overseas "communications" specialists brought to this country by the State Department. The Brandeis globalism is embryonic but is developing on familiar lines — more foreign students, more foreign study, and more foreign operations, all supported by the foundations, the government, and private philanthropy.

As for Boston University, her chief distinction globally is her African Studies Program, one of the first two African centers established in this country — a decade ago — the other being at Northwestern. Since then, newer African centers — notably one at U.C.L.A., which is headed by a pupil of the Harvard scholar Rupert Emerson — have outstripped B.U.'s in size, but the latter is still very active. Of late it has been doing contract work for the U.S.A.I.D. program — briefing A.I.D. personnel about to leave for Africa, "debriefing" them on return, and getting up reading matter for them. Besides this it reinforces the B.U. curriculum, provides an African library, and attracts scholars here. Among those attracted are Africans, but the training of Americans is the main idea, according to Dr. Adelaide Hill, an American Negress at the center with whom I talked recently — I saw her in lieu of Dr. William Brown, the center's chief, who was away on a trip then. Dr. Hill comes from a scholarly family in Washington, D.C.; she has studied at Smith, Bryn Mawr, the University of Pennsylvania, and Radcliffe, where she got her Ph.D.; and she is married to an engineer, with a doctorate from M.I.T., who works in Cambridge. She told me that regional literature on all of Africa, with the exception of Egyptology, is well represented at the center. Also that African visitors to the U.S. like the idea of an African center in Boston — that it draws them to the community and makes them feel welcome here.

The African center is B.U.'s only such institution, but the place has a good share of foreign students and is also engaged in at least one foreign operation; a team of five B.U. scholars is trying, with U.S.A.I.D. support, to revive a school of public administration in Guinea. This school was started by the French when Guinea was in their empire, but was abandoned when the Guineans chose, on being freed, to stay out of the French Union of Africa and Madagascar. Since then it has languished through the various Guinean ups and downs, including the phase of Russian dominance there, but now the B.U. team hopes to get it going again. The task is thought a difficult one, but was undertaken after a survey mission, led by Dr. Hubert S. Gibbs, chairman of B.U.'s government department, went out and had a look at it.

The notes above pay little heed to the global cross-fertilization in Cambridge, which is considerable. Tufts and B.U. both have cross-registration with Harvard and M.I.T., which means that students from one place may take courses or use libraries at the others. Teachers, too, are borrowed back and forth — Brandeis, for instance, has good experts on Nigeria and Portuguese Africa, and the B.U. center calls them in to help indoctrinate A.I.D. personnel. Experts go to each other's seminars or colloquia and meet each other over drinks and dinner, and they trade ideas and stimulate each other. "I have students from the B.U. African program in my courses," said Raymond Vernon when I talked with him. "Also from Fletcher and M.I.T. I have friends, too, at M.I.T. and Fletcher, and we get together and talk things over. It all builds up." Or it amounts to a real tub of worms, as another Harvard professor has put it.

One institution in the region, though — Boston College, run by the Jesuits — is somewhat outside the interaction. When exploring Cambridge globalism I have found my way easily, as a rule, from place to place — the regional experts at Harvard or M.I.T. have been able to tell me whom I should see at Brandeis, B.U., or Tufts, and so have the public-relations people. But B.C. is out of the circle, according to my experience; the rest of the local Academe is vague about it, and B.C. students cross-register little, if at all. Perhaps it is a question of geography — B.C. being a mile or two south of the Charles, which in a way is the bottom of the Cambridge world — or perhaps it is cultural. Cambridge's globalism is dominated overwhelmingly by Wasp eggheads and Jewish intellectuals, groups that work well together in America today. Of course the mixture has liberal Catholics in it too, but not enough of them, perhaps, to make a bridge with B.C., whose background is Boston Irish and whose atmosphere has strong elements of religion and religious conservatism.

Whatever the reason, B.C. is apart from the Greater Cambridge global boom with its foundation money. Yet being a Jesuit college it is global in a way that antedates the current activity here. The Jesuits are a great missionary order, and the prime overseas interests of the Jesuits' New England province are Iraq and Jamaica. Most of the Jesuit

leaders in those places, I have been told, are B.C. graduates, and some of B.C.'s own teachers have returned here
after serving there. Beyond all that, B.C. is now exploring
things it can do in Latin America, and it has been training
a Peace Corps group for work in Lima. The college is
global all right, one gathers, but not quite Cambridge
global.

(B.C. also has better relations with the Greater Boston
populace and officialdom than do its sisters north of the
Charles (see page 184). It runs four or five seminars each
year on Boston economic problems, Boston city planning,
etc., which are attended by labor leaders, business leaders,
and others in the city's power structure. The seminars are
highly valued as a way of imparting new ideas to the community; and their director, Father Seavey Joyce, was also
recently made chairman, by Governor Endicott Peabody,
of the Metropolitan Area Planning Council, which does
planning for Greater Boston, a larger unit than the city
itself. Such local involvements of B.C., like its aloofness
from the fancier new globalism, express its different orien-
tation from that of the Cambridge world.)

The universities are not the only outfits in and around
Cambridge that deal in global political studies. A few of
the R & D firms on Route 128 do it too, as a sideline to their
main job. The two kinds of work are related, strange as it
may seem; in each case the firm maintains a group of scholars and sells their output to a bureau down in Washington.
But there is a difference in the kind of scholar maintained.
Instead of physicists or engineers, the teams are now composed of men like economists, sociologists, and regional
experts; and the true Cambridge academics usually rate
these "soft" scientists on 128 lower in quality than the
"hard" ones there. They find less of a career in it — the

engineers and physicists have more status on the Road and a better future there; it is more the thing to do in their community. And meanwhile a social scientist working full-time there is deprived of many normal academic rewards; he has no tenure, no students, and, if he is doing classified work, little chance to publish his findings. "Not publishing is very bad for a scholar," one M.I.T. professor has told me. "So is not teaching. Some people in these outer organizations go to great lengths to teach *a* course somewhere. There is a conflict in their motivation, you see. They didn't get their Ph.D. in a social science in order to work in a factory. The outer organizations pay more — some may pay double, say, the M.I.T. scale — but few here are interested." And so in this case 128 — with many exceptions, of course — draws on the marginal scholars.

Cambridge, as a matter of fact, isn't the best place to study this kind of soft-science contracting. Route 128 engages in it, but not eminently so far. Southern California, home of the vast and mysterious (to me) RAND Corporation, is a better example. "RAND is a professional shop," an M.I.T. globalist has told me, "that is oriented toward the Air Force and toward defense policy. It's much bigger, for instance, than our Center for International Studies. And our center has lots of graduate students working in it too. RAND has no students and no teaching, though some of the people in it do teach a little at, say, U.C.L.A." One big 128 firm, I have been told by an expert, set out deliberately a few years ago to imitate, and compete with, the RAND Corporation in political studies. It hasn't made too good a showing, and one wonders if Cambridge's conservatism hasn't hindered it. Perhaps the bizarre atmosphere of Southern California is better for the launching of these farther-out activities.

There is another organized way, at any rate, for the Cambridge soft scientists to find employment. I know one agency near Harvard Square — and there may well be others — that hires them to work on contract studies for U.S. business firms and government departments. It is called Associates for International Research, Inc., which shortens nicely into AIRINC and thus satisfies the rules of modern Cambridge nomenclature. Its chief is a tall young man named James Boyce — a graduate of the Fletcher School who has also worked for the U.S. government in Southeast Asia — and among its directors is Max Millikan. AIRINC was founded a decade ago, and most of its work is now done for private business firms, though originally the government was the main thing.

"We used to have an office in New York as well," Boyce has told me. "That was convenient — it was near our principal clients — but when we decided to locate in only one spot Cambridge was the obvious choice. Cambridge is especially good because of the high quality of graduate-school labor here — on the research-assistant level, that is. The use of professors is a little on the wane now. A decade ago, and more, the professors here were hungry, but now they've been getting extended grants and fellowships. And they're in general demand as consultants too. So they tend to overprice themselves. They are hard to hire for large amounts of time, though they are still good for part-time employment — often their main contribution is in ideas, anyway, for which you don't need full-time. Cambridge is still good for that sort of thing, and it's just superlative for graduate assistants, the kind you hire for two and a half to three and a half dollars an hour. We have six or seven on our payroll now who are aiming at Ph.D.'s. They like the chance to work on real problems — our only true competition is from paper-grading jobs in the schools themselves. We have the pick of students in the Harvard Russian center, and we take them from the Social Relations department and the Business School as well."

I asked what kind of jobs the firm specialized in. "Just before you came to my office," Boyce answered, "I was working on an evaluation of the salary difference a company should pay when transferring an employee from Hong Kong to Tokyo. And this afternoon I hope to send off material to Brussels on another compensation question. Meanwhile I am getting ready to fly down to Bogotá, the day after tomorrow, to study the Colombian inflation for a Chicago firm. I expect to be there a week; it's much easier to go there myself than to try and do the job by mail."

I asked about AIRINC's government work, and Boyce said some of it has been done for A.I.D.; the firm makes feasibility studies of A.I.D. projects and also reports sometimes on the efficiency of A.I.D.'s own operations (rather in the manner, I gathered, of the recent Clay report, though on a smaller scale). Then there is a series of contracts with the Air Force, not wholly classified, that has gone on for several years and that deals, at least in part, with the rate and direction of technological change in Russia. I didn't ask which Cambridge experts had been helping with this work. But I know, of course, that Alexander Korol — whose boss at M.I.T., Max Millikan, is also a director of AIRINC — is a student of Russian technology; and I also know that Alex Inkeles, a senior research associate with AIRINC, is a key man in Harvard's Russian center (and helped it do mass interviewing of Russian refugees — delving into technology among other things — on an Air Force contract in the early 'fifties). I guess therefore, and I believe not wrongly, that AIRINC has been able to enlist those talents for the work. Also that it has been able to organize the job in a way acceptable to the Air Force, which the universities themselves might have found difficult. Harvard, for one thing — or the Harvard Russian center — would have had to refuse the classified part of the undertaking.

Of course Harvard's globalists may take classified work as individuals, in a free-lance way, and no doubt some do. Perhaps some of all the Cambridge globalists do. Secrets are secrets, and there is no way of finding out. Nor can one find to what degree the various Cambridge global centers, and global operations, have themselves been taken over by *sub rosa* workers — or have even been set up originally, as covers, by such people. This is always a question when one is looking into foundations or development projects or the like. One must assume that they may be false fronts, or may have been penetrated by our intelligence unbeknownst to their managements, or may even have been penetrated by a foreign intelligence. One must assume, in short, that the gentle Cambridge scene may mask a good deal else. Then one must forget about the matter, since prying into secrets goes badly with the Cold War effort.

All that aside, anyway, the number of Cambridge academics doing government work on their own is large. A recent story in the Boston *Globe,* not seriously contradicted that I know of, estimated that from eight hundred to a thousand of Harvard's fifty-six hundred faculty members with Corporation appointments held government jobs of one kind or another. The writer noted some indications of the number's vastness — the fact, for instance, that a minor wreck had revealed the presence of thirty-eight Harvard professors on a train heading, in 1957, for the Eisenhower inaugural — but he granted that exact figures could not be had: even the Harvard administration disclaimed knowledge of them (saying, as usual, that what a professor does with his own time is his own business). Presumably M.I.T., which says that a professor may spend one day a week on private affairs, is at least as lenient. If one counts in Brandeis, B.U., and the others, one gets a total, for senior Cambridge academics on the federal rolls, that must approach two thousand. Many of the number would be scientists, and not a few would be economists or law professors, but of globalists there would be several hundred anyway. Often they travel on government business, and then the foundations put uncounted others on the road. The Ford Foundation, especially, is legendary in Cambridge now. I know one professor here who has traveled a good deal on Ford money; he looks piously at the ceiling and speaks of "the Ford Foundation, the source of all good things," whenever he mentions it. And another professor, when telling me recently of a colleague's global operations, said "so he dashed off to the Ford Foundation and got some money" rather as an earlier raconteur might have said "he dashed off to the stable and got a horse." And so the sky is full now of academics with their briefcases.

There is another side, of course, to all this orbiting. In the 'fifties I worked as a journalist in underdeveloped countries, and often then I dreaded the appearance of airborne scholars. I felt that many of them really knew little, and perhaps cared little, about the lands I was studying so fondly — that they came seeking, instead, to fit them into preconceived hypotheses. Then more recently, while living in Cambridge, I have been forgetting that idea. In their home habitat the professors have seemed so urbane — so cultivated, so intelligent — that I have begun doubting my doubts of them. I have been of two minds, and so I was glad last winter when an old friend, an American whose time is spent mainly in grass-roots fraternization with Southeast Asians, came through here on a trip. His thoughts, I suspected, would be much like mine if I had stayed in Asia, and so I asked about them.

"Tell me," I said. "We used to view with horror the arrival of scholars flying in on planes. Do you still do that?"

"Horror has changed to amusement," he said, "but often the complaint is much the same — the scholars are lost in a verbal wonderland. Sometimes I think this is the greatest trap now facing American civilization. We create a verbal scheme of what we think the world is, then we go out and look for evidence to fit it. Last summer I was talking with an American friend in a Far Eastern city; he has lived there twenty-five years. We were discussing another friend, an able professor at a university here in the States, who had just been making a survey in that area. 'He's an attractive man,' my friend there said. 'He's very intelligent, and very concerned about the world, but you know he's been asking the wrong questions. They've been projected from his view of reality, and their relationship to what really matters here has been only tangential.' You remember how it is in Asia" — my friend said with, I thought, a look of doubt — "you remember that the truth is the last thing people there will tell you. They will tell it only when they trust you, when they know you so intimately that they can stake their careers on your discretion. And that kind of relationship is never built up on this fly-by-night basis." My friend poured himself a drink. "In many ways," he said, "the airplane has been a step backward. Before Pearl Harbor, when someone went to the Far East he had to stay long enough to get the feel of the place. But now he just drops in, and maybe out again in thirty-six hours. You know a lot of these people are intellectual freeloaders. They've got a grant to make a summer trip around the world — for the government or the universities or the foundations — and they want to bring home something fresh. So they pick up whatever pieces go with their verbal schemes, without really checking on the realities. I think our troubles in Asia come largely from this process."

No doubt my friend put it too strongly. No doubt he suffers from a weakness — the parochialism of the Old China Hand — that is complementary to that of the professors. But still his words rang a bell with me. While in Asia I had developed my own thoughts, parallel to his, about the theoreticalness of our view. I had thought our view of Asians particularly *abstract,* and I had linked this with our bias toward technology. I had compared it with what I conceived to be the old British view of Asians (or Asiatics, as they called them). This latter view had come, in my belief, from the close relationship of the upper-class British with horses and other animals, a relationship that had taught them, from childhood on, to regard their fellow beings as possessed of quirks that were essentially illogical but that could be understood well enough through experience and intuition, and could then be dealt with — curbed or exploited — as wisdom seemed to decree. To my mind our American childhood, in contrast, is spent much more with machines, which has been leading us to regard foreigners, or foreign social groups, essentially as mechanisms that can be dealt with in a logical way — according, one might say, to a machine manual. No doubt my analysis has flaws, but it does help explain some obvious facts, like the prominence of the social sciences in our approach to life. We *are* abstract in our view of other peoples, especially of underdeveloped peoples. This is true of our nation as a whole, in my experience, and truer still of our academics, to whom words on paper, after all — in books, in libraries, in Ph.D. theses — are the very stuff of life.

To say it another way, the Cambridge globalists — with many exceptions, of course — are subjective in their outlook, however much they may claim objectivity. They see things from the "liberal" intellectual viewpoint. They have a scholar mentality and are bound by scholar ethics. By and large they are men who long ago — say in their teens — chose to be thinkers, not doers. In middle age, thanks to this Cambridge renaissance, they may take a belated flyer at doing — as scholar-entrepreneurs, or government advisers, or Point Four field workers — but only if the conditions are right, a proviso that is all important. I was in Cambridge when the phrase "Point Four" was first given currency. That was in President Truman's second inaugural address, in January of 1949. Truman was ticking off a list of promises — "Point One . . ., Point Two . . ., Point Three . . ." — and Point Four was about using our technology to advance the backward areas. I don't think the idea meant much to Truman or his Administration; at least they didn't hurry to set up a Point Four office in Washington — even by the following June they had done little in that line. But in Cambridge the President's words were hailed as a new dispensation. Academe went wild over the idea, and it still is wild, according to what I have seen here. Point Four is to a Cambridge globalist like catnip to a cat, and I have spent much time, since 1949, in wondering why. I have speculated that the globalists of '49 were especially frustrated — with our China policy going against them, with McCarthyism in the offing and so on — and that they wanted a safe line to work in, which Point Four was. I have also speculated that their Point Four zeal released

national do-good energies that had previously been chan-
neled off through our Christian missionary movement — I
have even wondered if Truman's happy phrase "Point
Four" might not have conjured up thoughts of the cross
itself from our subconscious. And I have made other specu-
lations too.

They have never quite given the full answer, but I was
helped further toward this, last spring, by a professor here.
I was discussing Cambridge globalism in general with him,
and I mentioned the rage I had noticed for Point Four.
"I feel somehow," I said, "that Point Four's attraction
here doesn't lie in its usefulness alone. Development work
may be of crucial importance, or it may not, but I feel the
scholars would be keen on it anyway. Their keenness seems
to be subjective, almost tribal."

The professor smiled. "Perhaps they see an opportunity
in it," he said. "Intellectuals respond to opportunities too,
you know — not just to challenges and duties."

"You mean opportunities to travel?" I asked. "Opportunities to get grants?"

"Opportunities to work on something intellectualizable," he answered. "If a national problem can be intel-
lectualized, the academics will respond to it. They responded to the Hoover Commission, for instance, which
was studying ways to reorganize the government; they were
enthusiastic about that. And they are responding to our
defense problems now for the same reason; those problems
are intellectualizable. The development problem is the
same. Historically, you know, the government always attracts more academic intellectuals when it is stressing
welfare. The Wilson administration attracted a great many
— especially, where foreign affairs are concerned, when it
was working out the peace and the postwar world."

Academic ethics are tricky, as can be seen through another look at the Harvard–M.I.T. comparison. A professor at M.I.T. may serve as readily, perhaps, in business
as in government, but to a Harvard one the government
service comes easier; Harvard professors, especially Business School professors, *may* serve in business under certain
conditions, but it isn't done throughout their community
as at M.I.T. Yet why should a job in a government agency
be nobler, essentially, than a job in a factory making arms
for a government agency? One hears Harvard professors
dignifying government jobs with talk of duty — of "when
the nation needs us we can't refuse" — but this doesn't give
the whole picture. A different idea can be had from a story
I was told last winter by a Harvard law professor. "After
Kennedy's election in 1960," the professor said, "there was
a strong feeling in the Law School here against Bobby
Kennedy's being made Attorney General. The Law School
is influential in Washington, as you know, and a move was
begun here to get up a petition on the point. Various men
on the Law School faculty were approached. Most of them
were for the petition, it turned out, but some of the leading
ones were reluctant to sign it. They were hoping, you see,
that the new lightning down in Washington would strike
them, and they didn't want to queer their chances. In the
end the petition had to be dropped, for lack of really first-
class support." Many Harvard professors, including some of
the best, are really avid for Washington, yet one can hardly
suspect them of being avid for business careers. Their
group mentality is against that. This mentality has been
much influenced by the many Harvard professors, past and
present — mainly in the humanities — who have sub-
scribed to European ideals of the secluded, aristocratic
scholarly life. To be in trade does not fit those ideals. Such

men are but a small minority at M.I.T., on the other hand. They do exist there, and criticisms of the M.I.T. rage for business — often couched in terms of "conflict of interest" — are heard nowadays at the Institute. But the criticisms don't prevail, and "trade" is allowed by M.I.T.'s overall ethical scheme. That scheme, like Harvard's, is established by a consensus of the community, and once established is more or less binding on the members.

The ethics of making *arms* is another thing that the consensus — of Harvard, of M.I.T., of Cambridge as a whole — must worry about these days. The arms business on Route 128, and Cambridge's involvement in it, has been criticized here on many grounds — that there is graft and laxity in the letting of government contracts; that the new money is distorting academic values here; that Cambridge talents are being wasted in "technological leaf-raking" on 128; and so on. But the worst sin, by academic standards, is that scholars are themselves engaged here in the munitions trade, an activity that a mere quarter century ago, on the eve of the Second World War, was regarded as heinous by our intellectuals almost to a man. In those days Schneider-Creusot and Sir Basil Zaharoff were the great devils; now the devil is more apt to be the Pentagon — the image of an America fast coming under domination by military men and militarism is a real one to many thoughtful people here. They would like to struggle against the domination, yet they see themselves, or their institutions, implicated in it — they see their community compromised, right and left, by military patronage. Some academics bow to the new situation; some continue to fight it stubbornly. David Riesman, now a professor of social sciences at Harvard, attacks it in a publication, *Council for Correspondence,* that is modeled on our pre-Revolutionary Committee of Correspondence. Various Cambridge scientists have also attended the Pugwash Conferences, aimed at relaxing the Cold War, in the past few years. And student peace movements are encouraged here by Riesman and others; recently I went to a peace conference at Boston University where several Cambridge professors held forth and where one *non*-Cambridge professor pointed in M.I.T.'s direction and complained about the amount of federal money the Institute is accepting. These gestures may not change the situation, but they do express a restlessness in the academic psyche.

Such restlessness is plentiful now, much of it engendered by Cambridge's new power in the world. A young Harvard scholar was discussing it all with me the other day. "Look how acquisitive the universities here are," he said. "Look how they collect things. Harvard's library is the third largest in America, and its Chinese-Japanese library is the largest outside the Far East. But still they keep on growing. Look at the university presses and the journals — the paper that comes out of this community — the fantastic ribbon of paper between here and other institutions, spreading influence. Look at all the learned societies, with their annual meetings here and there. Lots of communication at *them* — mainly about job-finding, it is true, but about other things as well. So-and-so" — he named an eminent professor of history — "travels to two or three of these meetings every year — one for his discipline, one for his regional specialty, and so on. And he makes innumerable trips to the foundations. Think of the tug-of-war between administration and teaching now. All this growth in Cambridge means more administration throughout. How big is Harvard's bureaucracy now, how big is its maintenance staff? Does anybody know? I wonder."

Much is being said now — in this and other veins — against the new activities. But the saying is hardly apt to change things, for the new élite here, with all its peculiarities, is well established. It can be seen as a new caste, not unlike the Brahmin caste of India. Metaphorically the Brahmins are supposed to form the head of the Indian community, while the Kshatriyas, or warrior caste, form its arms — the workers forming the legs and so on. The Brahmins and Kshatriyas have been complementary, in the old tradition — unable to get along without each other. The Kshatriyas, men of action, have made good rulers, but only if they have had Brahmins to instruct them. And so it is today with the Johnsons and McNamaras, not to mention the Khrushchevs; without their Brahmins they are helpless. Now the old Indian Brahmins have often been bad people — parasitic, hypocritical, negatively intellectual, and so on. But this hasn't harmed them greatly; they have run India for thousands of years despite it; not even the centuries of Buddhist dominance there could get them out. Our own new élite may have its faults, but it seems really less deplorable, so far, than the old Brahmins were — some would call it automatically better because it is recruited by competition, not by birth. In this it is like — to change our model — the Chinese mandarinate, another durable group, which was always replenished through scholarly examinations. That group was limited, pretty much, to sons of the well-to-do — who could afford sufficient education — and it attracted opportunists more often than altruists, but still it endured. Our own new élite is showing signs of opportunism, too, in its younger echelons, and it may get worse in that regard. But even this will hardly fell it, for we *need* the scholars so. We can't defend our country without them, we can't run our economy without them, we can't even attempt a foreign policy without them. Next to technological force, technological aid is our main binder for the Free World now, and it can't conceivably be applied without technologists.

COMPUTERS

V IN DISCUSSING the personnel of Cambridge's renaissance one must not overlook computers, which have
entrenched themselves in parts of the academic world and
become indispensable there. When I lived in Cambridge
before, near Harvard Square, I heard vaguely of a Professor Norbert Wiener down at M.I.T., who was said to
have a thinking-machine engaged in something called
cybernetics; otherwise I was not aware of computers at all.
Today it is different. Wiener died a short while ago; the
word cybernetics is fading from the jargon here; but computers as a race have arrived. Both Harvard and M.I.T.
have big computer centers into which scholars feed problem after problem, working out new marriages between
machine calculation and American thought. The scholars
are teamed up with the computers rather as Erasmus was
teamed up with the printing-press, the great innovation of
his day, and are getting a comparable increase of power
thereby. With the computers' help they are designing
things, and studying other things, on a scale not dreamt of
in the past. One can almost see the computers — blessed

as they are with detachment, veracity, and other scholarly virtues — as a subcaste of the academic community. Indeed some Cambridge savants speak of "mechanical brains" and "artificial intelligence" in connection with them. Others decry this as "anthropomorphism" and call computers mere calculating-machines. And then there is a middle group who call them calculating-machines with other quasi-human abilities added — the ability to learn, for instance, and to remember, and to search through masses of data and find unsuspected patterns in it.

There is much discussion here about the machines, their natures, and their place in scholarly life. Harvard's President Pusey has stated cautiously that they help to conserve and advance knowledge, which he recognizes as a university function. Others say, more boldly, that they impose a helpful discipline on academic thought by refusing to handle problems that are loosely presented to them. Still others are seeking a better understanding of the human mind, and human society, by comparing them to computer operations. It is no exaggeration to call computers junior partners in much of the work being done here. Walter Rosenblith of M.I.T. says that "the combination of man plus computer bids fair to be the equivalent of a jump in the evolution of man's nervous system." Professor Rosenblith speaks with authority, for man's nervous system is the very thing he is using computers to explore.

Harvard and M.I.T. each claim the credit for having originated computers. History hasn't settled this question, but it is true at least that men from both places — like Professor Howard Aiken of Harvard and Professors Wiener and Vannevar Bush of M.I.T. — contributed greatly to the effort, which has also benefited from the defense money spent here, especially through M.I.T., in the Second

World War and later. Thanks to that history, Cambridge is now rivaled as a computer center by only a few places in the world (including Northern and Southern California and perhaps Yorktown Heights, near the Hudson, where IBM has its headquarters). Computers are not only playing a big part in academic thought here; they are also essential to the Cambridge world's prosperity as a munitions center.

M.I.T. and Harvard have somewhat different approaches to computers. Both places are doing work on machine translation, for instance, but while Harvard's courses in this field are listed in her catalogue under "Linguistics" and "Applied Mathematics," those of M.I.T. are listed under "Linguistics" and the more activist title of "Electrical Engineering." Harvard is relatively pure-science in her thinking about computers, M.I.T. is relatively mindful of their use in industry and defense. M.I.T. is also much more involved in the further development of computers themselves. In December 1962, Harvard founded a new computer center, with considerable help from IBM. This establishment serves all parts of the university and is sometimes compared to a library in its relationship with the whole. M.I.T. has long had such a center too (also in collaboration with IBM), but she is now moving into a new phase. Engineers are putting consoles in various parts of the M.I.T. premises, and these will be wired into the computer center so that people all through the Institute may use the latter without leaving their laboratories or offices. One hears this arrangement compared not so much to a library as to a public utility, say a telephone system. The arrangement is also linked with dreams of the future; and some at M.I.T. believe that whole cities, if not whole nations, will eventually be wired up to central computers in the same way. Meanwhile it is expected that many more of M.I.T.'s own faculty and students, inspired by the extension-consoles' existence, will learn to program and use the equipment; some even say that every graduate leaving the Institute after 1965 will know how to program. It is also expected that the center will handle much more business in the future, because computers themselves can calculate so fast; it is the programming and console work, now about to be diffused, that make for bottlenecks. The whole development (which is being supervised by Robert Fano, an M.I.T. professor) is seen here as a step toward a more computerized society.

Much of the computer work here is done in engineering and in the hard or quantifiable sciences, like physics and mathematics — the machines forever calculate the orbits of satellites, say, and the stresses in new bridges. That is a fairly old story. What is newer is the use of computers on the more quantifiable aspects of the soft sciences. I know one Harvard scholar who has been writing a book on Populism, and as part of this he has got a computer to analyze a mass of census material and voting records set down in Minnesota in the late nineteenth century. Another scholar here claims to have computed that the slave traffic, contrary to general belief, was a profitable business in the ante-bellum South — his procedure has been to comb through old Southern market records and other documents for hints about traffic, and then to use these as computer fodder. Another Cambridge couple, Professor Sheldon Glueck (of the Harvard Law School) and his wife Eleanor, have begun studying crime and juvenile delinquency by computer analysis of figures they have collected since the 1930's. Someone else, again, recently calculated word-frequencies in certain of the *Federalist* papers as a means of assigning their authorship to either Madison or Hamilton; Madison was declared the winner. And then one visiting psychologist here, last winter, did a computer study of an entire nine-session psychotherapy made by a psychiatrist several years ago and recorded by him verbatim in book form. In this study the text was fed into a machine programmed to add up various word-usages made by the patient and the psychiatrist throughout their nine sessions — also the changes in these frequencies as the sessions progressed. The machine plotted, for instance, the comparative frequency of the articles "the" and "a" in the speech of each party as time went on; also the changing frequency of conjunctions used by them; and so on. The investigating psychologist had believed that these small points of word frequency would prove symptomatic of the therapy's progress, and at the end he claimed to have charted its course reliably by analyzing them. He argues that in future, when the method has been perfected, it will help psychiatrists learn things about their seances that they would never detect through merely being present at them. This hope may or may not be realized, but anyway the psychologist's work is typical of much being done here — by historians, anthropologists, public-health experts, and many others. With the computers' help they are paying massive attention to small, specific details that may mean little singly, but that when plotted in a big way are expected to reveal larger, less tangible truths.

It would have been nice if the psychologist could have just handed the book to his machine and said "Read this." But in fact he needed a girl to punch the whole thing out on a tape. This was because of the scanning problem, or the difficulty of getting machines to read as we do, which still limits their usefulness in some ways. Experts here have told me that even the strange figures at the bottom of modern cheques, though dehumanized and printed in magnetic ink, are hard for machines to read; naturally, therefore, the reading of humanly acceptable characters is still *very* hard. Professor Anthony Oettinger, a Harvard linguist and computer expert, says that under the best conditions now a machine — or rather a scanning attachment for a machine — can read type from only one font and in only one size at a time. This is because scanning is usually done against a fine grid of light-points; and varying sizes, even if in perfect register, would confuse the scanner between such similar characters as O and Q. Oettinger has worked with Russian a good deal, and he says it is terribly hard to arrange machine-scanning of that language in printed form. This is partly because Russian documents suffer heavily from broken type, cheap paper, see-through, and general messiness, but even aside from this — even with capitalist printing — the problem is a hard one, and Oettinger expects no immediate easing of it. Professor Peter Elias, head of M.I.T.'s Department of Electrical Engineering, is more optimistic. He says the scanning problem hasn't been attacked on the proper scale yet; the investment has been too small and scattered — with paltry grants being squandered here and there on mere parts of the job, say the scanning of Russian specifically. Elias thinks that if the total enterprise were dealt with massively, by a varied team of experts commanding big government or foundation money, it would soon be mastered.

Linked with the scanning problem is another one, known to the experts here as that of information retrieval. Our culture is sometimes said to be undergoing a "knowledge explosion" now. The Cambridge renaissance, in fact, is one aspect of this. Another aspect is the great proliferation, in Cambridge and elsewhere, of scholarly writings on all manner of subjects. If one interviews many Cambridge professors, as I have done, one is given such a wealth of reprints, learned journals, mimeographed matter, and other forms of paper that one is nearly swamped; one must constantly rearrange one's files to take care of it all. But this personal problem is nothing compared to what the libraries are facing. They are deluged with new material and meanwhile are finding good help no easier to come by. Some librarians fear that their ability to index and to find or "retrieve" material will fail them; that the flood will simply get out of control. Under the circumstances, and with computers so prominent, suggestions are heard that it should all be done electronically. Some experts here say this is a pipe-dream — with the scanning art in its present state — but still it is talked about. Recently I heard a professor explain some of the non-scanning problems that retrieval of information is up against. "If a machine can read a mass of assorted documents," he said, "you can theoretically get it to make a note of any passage containing, say, the phrase 'police dogs.' That's fine, but then what about 'police *dog*'? Well, you can program for that too, of course, but it is a separate operation. Then you will probably want to catch any mention of, say, 'dogs used by the police.' You can program for that as well — you can get the machine to watch out for passages where the word 'dogs' is followed by the word 'police' at some reasonable interval. But then it will also record statements like 'the dogs howled while the police were raiding the cabin.' Humans solve these questions by a feeling for context, but machines can't do that."

Because of the scanning problem, some experts here believe that future publications will be recorded on tape, for storage, at the same time as they are put into print; a linotype machine could readily be made to punch a tape, for instance, as a by-product of manipulating its type-matrices. But this solution, as of now, is up against both the copyright laws and the unions. Copyright laws are already somewhat slighted in the Cambridge libraries, which often contain slot machines where for a quarter you can get a facsimile of any page you wish. This is piracy on a scale, and at a cost, that can apparently be winked at, but the possibility of vaster piracy from tape-libraries might well cause litigation. As for the unions, their fears about automation are well known. Machine enthusiasts in the local universities argue that the great increase of computers in the Cambridge region has not hurt labor. They say that a good deal of transitory, low-paid girlpower has indeed been displaced — in the plants on Route 128, for instance — but that higher-paid male technicians and programmers have been taken on in almost equal number. Also that the sizable computer-*manufacturing* industry here has absorbed many unemployed workers from the old textile mills near by. These facts may all be true of the Cambridge world, which is a sort of computer paradise, but they seem hardly general enough to mollify labor about what strikes it as an overall, national threat.

Besides merely calculating, in the hard sciences or the soft, computers are used here a lot for "simulation." This is a vogue-word whose popularity is criticized by some local purists. It means the programming of a computer to imitate a real-life situation — the making of a "mathematical model," as the experts say, to fit that situation — and then programming new elements into it, experimentally, in hopes of telling what the future may bring when approached in various ways. A man's budget is a model of his finances. He can program contemplated actions into it — the purchase, say, of an airplane — and the budget will show where this will leave him without his having to buy the plane experimentally. Computer simulation is much the same, but can deal with infinitely more complex processes. Some critics here object that computers don't simulate the processes themselves, but only hypotheses about them. Others say that computers no more simulate processes than did our childhood mathematical operations — the only difference is that they can handle more variables. In algebra you can take a formula with two variables — say x and y — and chart, on graph paper, the parabola of a bridge cable. With a computer, by taking in dozens of variables, you can come close to charting the behavior of a whole economic system. The critics say this ability is merely an extension of the old mathematics and doesn't deserve a fancy title, but even so the phrase "computer simulation" seems here to stay — it has proved useful, for one thing, in the sales talk of those who offer computer services commercially.

Not long ago M.I.T. staged a conference on the computer simulation of social and political processes. Twenty or thirty experts were on the conference list to start with, but in the end some fifty came, and more would have liked to. At one point in the proceedings Ithiel de Sola Pool, an M.I.T. professor who had helped arrange the conference, asked all those present what they were currently working on. No less than twenty-two reported that they were engaged in the computer simulation of one thing or another — business problems, international politics, national economies, political campaigns, "communications" processes, and so on. "Simulation" is plainly a rage here. It is being

done not only on the Cambridge campuses, but also in the
nearby spin-off firms, like Raytheon and MITRE, on
Route 128 (not to mention such distant, and reputedly very
busy, outfits as the RAND Corporation and *its* spin-off, the
Systems Development Corporation, in Southern California). Both the Harvard Business School and the M.I.T.
Sloan School of Management are deeply involved in teaching, and experimenting with, computer simulation as a
guide to businessmen. The title of a book just put out by
the Harvard school — *New Decision-Making Tools for
Managers; Mathematical Programming as an Aid in the
Solving of Business Problems* — gives an idea of that organization's interests. As for the M.I.T. school, it has a
great pioneer of business simulation in Professor Jay Forrester, an electrical engineer who formerly guided M.I.T.'s
development of Whirlwind I, an early high-speed computer, and of the SAGE warning net for defense against
missiles. In 1956 Dr. Forrester suddenly began applying
his concepts of electrical engineering to business management, working out a system that he calls "Industrial Dynamics" — he has described it in a book of that name.
With the help of mathematics and computers he simulates
the flow of goods, orders, and other elements through an
industrial firm and thereby discovers — or so he maintains
— unsuspected, and even surprising, ways of increasing
efficiency. He did a study for one client, the Sprague
Electric Company of North Adams, Mass., which suggested that an erratically fluctuating employment rate then
troubling the company was caused by customer reaction to
its inventory policy. This was almost the last thing the
management would have guessed, but with some reserva-
tions they took Forrester's advice, and are said not to
regret it.

Ithiel Pool is another M.I.T. professor who engages in computer simulation as a business. Pool is not an engineer, but a social scientist, on the staff of M.I.T.'s Center for International Studies; he has specialized there in international "communications" problems. His researches have grown increasingly computerized, and in 1959 he helped found a firm called the Simulmatics Corporation, whose main offices are in New York (he is now the chairman of its board). According to Pool — a tall, dark, pleasant young man with a Madison Avenue air — Simulmatics offers to do any desired application of computer simulation in the social sciences. It is, for instance, simulating the Venezuelan economy now for a Venezuelan government agency. And before and during the 1960 presidential campaign it simulated alternative strategies of various kinds for the Democratic Party — computing what would happen, for instance, if Kennedy met the religious issue forthrightly or otherwise. A main current project of Simulmatics — and one managed by Dr. Pool himself — is a service for advertisers called Media-Mix. This aims at predicting, by simulation of American audiences, just who will be reached, and how often and efficiently, by various combinations of advertisements in magazines, newspapers, radio programs, and so on. To that end it will use thumbnail biographies of 2944 hypothetical Americans that have been put on magnetic tape — with details of where they live, how they live, what they do, what they read, and what they are interested in. These people will not be the real public, or even a living sample of the public, such as the Gallup Poll uses; instead they will be a fictional sample undertaking to be typical, and their only existence will be in the computer's memory. On this imaginary group the computer will try out various "mixes" of advertising. It will know what each member of its hypothetical public is doing at every minute of the day, and it can quickly say what percentage of ears will be reached by a radio program at a given hour. Or it can say, almost as quickly, what percentage will be reached by a nightly program throughout the ensuing year, and what the cumulative effect will be. The results of a real-life poll are transitory, because people's minds keep changing, but with Media-Mix the model will keep changing too — by having new influences programmed into it — and will theoretically be always fresh. The system can hardly work unless the programs are realistic, but Dr. Pool maintains that his have already proven out well in actual tests.

It must be stressed that Simulmatics is only a sideline of Dr. Pool's. He teaches courses in political science at M.I.T., and with two other scholars he recently published a 490-page book on American attitudes toward foreign trade and tariffs. He also has interests that are more academic still, in the sense of not being immediately practical. For some time he has been studying what he calls the "small world" question; he has been trying to find out what the chances are of any two people, chosen at random, having a friend in common. For this purpose he gets a great many subjects to keep lists of everyone they talk with over a period of time; then he circulates the lists for others to check any cross-acquaintanceships; and then he analyzes the results. By now he has reached the belief that if you take two American census cards at random, the chances are better than even that the two people they stand for will have at least a friend of a friend in common. And he thinks that any two Americans, of any sort, can be linked by a chain of six acquaintanceships or less.

Dr. Pool enjoys this kind of pure science — a mathematical study of the social fabric, it might be called — but at the same time he makes no apology for the attention he gives to applications. He thinks applied work is a boon to the social sciences because it makes possible types of research that would be out of the question otherwise. He says half the best communications research to date has been done for the armed forces — on problems of morale, indoctrination, etc. — where scholars have been given huge samples to work with. He thinks Simulmatics offers a comparable opportunity.

Harvard professors keep clear, on the whole, of things like Simulmatics, but still Harvard is engaged in one of the biggest simulation jobs yet attempted for social-service ends. This is the simulation of West Pakistan's Indus Valley waters with a view to controlling them, getting the most out of them, and reclaiming vast areas of soil that they have waterlogged and made saline. The Indus tributaries and the plain they flow through — the Punjab or "Five Rivers" — have been the greatest scene of irrigation, perhaps, in man's career. Scholars now believe that "hydraulic" civilizations, based on irrigation, have been very widespread and go back far into prehistoric times. Modern high-altitude photography, from planes and satellites, has been showing up traces of big ancient irrigation systems hitherto unsuspected by us — they have been found in Arizona, for instance — and this has fostered a belief that some old hydraulic civilizations may have vanished, Heaven knows how long ago, without leaving *any* trace.

It is impossible, therefore, to say when irrigation of the Punjab began. But we do know that an advanced culture, emphasizing water, flourished there at least as early as the third millennium B.C. — remains of this culture, including water conduits, have been found at the site of Mohenjo-

Daro, near the Indus's present course. That old Indus
Valley Civilization — for so it is called — fell long before
the dawn of history, but since then the plain has remained
important; it was, for instance, the eastern edge of Alexander's empire, and later the route by which the Moguls
conquered India. Then, in the nineteenth century, the
British began a huge irrigation scheme in the Punjab, the
biggest ever undertaken anywhere. With a network of
canals they watered more than twenty million acres, popu-
lating this area with a whole new overlay of towns and
villages. The Punjab became the bread-basket of India, a
great asset to the Empire's economy. As such it prospered
lushly for decades, but then it began, in places, to go bad:
the soil grew salty there, and marshy — it would not drain
well, and gradually it ceased producing. The Punjab was
facing the doom that may have ended many hydraulic
cultures, for waterlogging and salinity, it now appears,
often result from irrigation that raises the water-table under the plain concerned. In most of the Punjab, before
irrigation, the water-table was fifty or seventy feet below
the surface. But the new British canals, which chanced to
be cut through porous earth, leaked much new water down
on top of this. The level of wells in the Punjab began to
rise; then ground-water began drowning the root-zones in
some places; and elsewhere the surface water, brought by
irrigation, could no longer sink down in — it had to lie on
top till it escaped by evaporation, leaving its poisonous salts
behind. This very process, scholars now believe, had attacked many settlements of antiquity; but on the Indus
plain it was especially bad because the undertaking was so
big there — with such a vast new population — and so
many other regions depended on it.

So it was into a classic predicament that Harvard's computers and computer experts were thrown, and the way this was done was also classic. President Kennedy and President Ayub Khan of Pakistan, the two chiefs of state, were talking one day — on July 14, 1961 — in Washington. Their talk was pleasant and informal, and toward the end of it Kennedy asked Ayub if there was anything special he could do for him. Yes, said Ayub hopefully, he could perhaps do something about the Indus Valley, on which West Pakistan depended and which was failing (it was losing, to be exact, an acre every five minutes from production). Kennedy responded by calling in his wise men. Jerome Wiesner of M.I.T., the chief of his Scientific Advisory Council, happened to be away at the moment, but Harvey Brooks of Harvard, the Council's deputy chief, was in town and available, and also acquainted with some computer studies that Harvard scholars had been making of river systems. Backed by the Rockefeller Foundation, these scholars — a mixed team of political scientists, economists, and hydraulic engineers — had been working out the simulation of rivers in general as a guide to flood control, pollution control, and the proper use of water for things like irrigation and power. They had been thinking of American rivers primarily, but their programs were abstract and could be applied to the Indus with some further work. So in September, after a period of rather loose discussions in Washington, a ten-man team settled down at Harvard to solve the problem. These American experts knew what was basically wrong with the Indus — knew that to save the land they must lower the water-table — and the question they faced was how to do it. They began to simulate remedies — the lining of canals, the installation of tubewells to get the ground-water out — all on a vast and costly scale. They simulated different spacing of wells, and different rates of pumping, and computed the water-tables, year by year, that would result. They needed data on rainfall, and on the rivers' rates of flow, and they got this from Pakistan and India and London; the British, luckily, had kept good records in their years of rule. As the data came in, the team made up its specific model of the Indus, a job that took five months before it was properly adjusted. Meanwhile a subteam, of four mathematicians, worked out two theoretical problems — about the behavior of salt in water flowing through soil — that had not been hitherto solved and that stood in the way; this took four months and millions of computer calculations.

Finally, in March of 1962, the team made its recommendation: that the Punjab be fitted out with tubewells at the rate of a million contiguous acres a year — going by such big areas so that neighboring ground-water couldn't readily flow into them and keep the table up. A modern electric-power system — using natural gas, which is plentiful in the region — was also recommended, as was a big project for using the gas to make fertilizers. Washington approved the plan, and the Harvard experts went off to tell Pakistan about it. Meanwhile, though, they had decided that the effort would be wasted unless the Pakistanis also resolved to double farm production, by an all-round Point Four attack, in each of the reclaimed areas within five years. They persuaded the Pakistanis of this, and the latter have already reorganized their government to make the effort. Meanwhile the Harvard people have been computing about diets, crop programs, and the educating of Pakistani farmers into changing their ways. They are, in short, deep in social planning by simulation. Their Indus project, whose working out has been financed by U.S.A.I.D., is the most ambitious development plan America has ever urged on an underdeveloped country. It is revolutionary for Pakistan and revolutionary, too, for theories of development, in that it concentrates on agriculture instead of industrialization. It is a big venture all around, as befits the Punjab's place in history. Yet thanks to computers it was devised by a few academics amid the Harvard bricks and ivy.

As sweeping and radical, though in a different way, is the use that Walter Rosenblith puts computers to. Professor Rosenblith has worked with scientists as disparate as Norbert Wiener, the cybernetics man, and Dr. Georg von Békésy, a Hungarian-born scientist at Harvard who won a Nobel Prize in 1961 for his work on the physics of hearing. Professor Rosenblith — a vivacious *Austrian*-born scientist — is a "communications biophysicist" at M.I.T. and studies the activities of the nervous system in general — especially its sensory aspects — by linking it up electrically with a computer and letting the latter help him observe it. Scientists have studied brain electricity for several decades now, and since the 1920's they have been drawing off electrical activity — "brain-waves" — through electrodes placed on the skull or within the brain itself and recording them in "electro-encephalograms." But the brain electricity is so complex — each single theme in it is so confused by extraneous "noise" — that they have had trouble isolating chosen parts of it. Professor Rosenblith and others have found that the data-processing abilities of computers can help in this. By causing many repetitions of the same phenomenon — the response of a subject's brain, say, to a given sight or sound — and running the electric records through a computer, they can get the latter to "average" them — to superimpose them on each other — and bring

out patterns not detectable in a single run. Or they can
use the computer's pattern-discerning skill in other ways —
always to spot order in the apparent chaos. Professor Rosenblith likens the computer, indeed, to the microscope or
telescope in its value as a research tool. Much of its suita-
bility comes from the fact that brain and computer have
electricity pulsing through them in rather similar ways.
And it is also lucky, Rosenblith says, that he is working at
M.I.T., where computers have been developed especially
for use in military warning nets like SAGE and the DEW-
line. The brain behaves, he explains, more like such net-
works than it does like the computer systems designed, say,
for business purposes; its activity is hard to assess in the
precise numbers that go on punch-cards in a business
system — it is more akin to the vaguer patterns or "relationships" that are expressed in electric impulses.

Be that as it may, Professor Rosenblith has been helped
enthusiastically, and creatively, by some of M.I.T.'s electrical engineers, especially those connected with the Lincoln Laboratory, where the warning nets were developed.
One of these engineers, Wesley Clark, Jr., has been designing machines expressly for biological use — especially he
has put together one called the ARC, or average-response
computer, which excels at the averaging mentioned above.
He has also been developing a small machine called the
LINC, or laboratory-instrument computer, which is in-
tended for "biomedical" researchers to use on their own,
without the help of programmers or technicians.

Rosenblith's situation brings out the difference between
Harvard's and M.I.T.'s way with computers. However
imaginatively Harvard may use computers — whether for
simulation, mere calculation, or what — she gets the actual
machines from the outside. M.I.T., on the other hand,

often makes them, and the engineers that do it are right there, working with Professors Rosenblith and Pool and other academic users, as well as with the military that does so much to support their efforts. Rosenblith calls himself, jokingly, a profiteer of the Cold War, and he says that in his work the life sciences are getting massive benefits from technology for the first time. His own laboratory, appropriately, is in the midst of M.I.T.'s Research Laboratory for Electronics, surrounded there by physicists and engineers. And his staff is fully interdisciplinary, with Ph.D.'s in mathematics, physics, electrical engineering, psychology, and physiology all working together.

When I went to see Dr. Rosenblith, he showed me an experiment that a colleague, Dr. Robert Hall, was doing in his laboratory. It was aimed at exploring the electricity of a rat's responses to a light flashed at it, again and again, while the rat was also engaged in a learning process. The rat was in a darkened box — we could watch it through a hole in the top — and it had three wires attached to its head; one was a ground, I was told, and the other two led to a computer from visually-important regions of the rat's brain. The rat was being trained — and was well along in the process — to press down a lever, which would cause a bright light to shine in its eyes, and then to hold the lever down for just two seconds; if it did this correctly a food-pellet would drop into a container behind it. The rat was performing well — repeatedly, in a steady rhythm, it flashed its light, turned to eat its food, and turned back to its lever again. We watched it awhile, then closed the box top, brightened the room lights, and looked at the equipment that the rat was wired to. In addition to the computer the electric impulses went to an oscilloscope, on whose TV-like screen they appeared as fleeting blue-green dots and flashes. They looked enigmatic to me, and I gathered that even a practiced researcher could get from them only a rough idea of what was happening. But once in the computer the same impulses could be averaged, analyzed, and otherwise processed into readable form. They could also be stored on tapes for future processing — there was a library of such tapes in the next room: shelves of them, in cases, lining the walls there. With the help of computers the records on them could be combined with those from other experiments too, and knowledge of how information travels through the nervous system could be generalized and built up systematically.

The brain-computer similarity, such as it may be, is exploited here in other ways, too. Some researchers simulate individual nerve cells with transistors or vacuum tubes, then hook these up in various ways to simulate the workings of nerve *tissues*. Others program more complex mental processes into full-fledged computers. A recent visitor at the Harvard Center for Cognitive Studies, a Japanese professor, tried while there a simulation of a hypothetical robot living very simply on a distant planet; its chief activities were to eat fungus and mine uranium. The robot made decisions by machine computation, and one aim of the study was to explore the limits of this — to find if there was any other possible way of decision-making or if the robot was trapped in an endless chain of computing whether to compute whether to compute, and so on. The issue was still unresolved at last reports, and meanwhile other Cambridge experimenters have been trying machines out on such mental exercises as chess-playing and the manipulation of symbols in formal logic.

The computers' greatest field of brain-work, perhaps, is

in linguistics. There is a whole movement of scholars here, divided between Harvard and M.I.T., whose work relates to this. There are the machine-translation experts themselves, led by Harvard's Anthony Oettinger and M.I.T.'s Victor Yngve. There is the mathematical grammarian Noam Chomsky at M.I.T., whose work on syntax has opened up new approaches for machines and humans as well. And there is the Harvard psychologist George Miller, whose experiments have shed light on human limitations — and by inference machine limitations — in the handling of grammatical complexities. These men, and others, give each other ideas, confirmations, and encouragement to a degree that warrants their being called a school. And behind them all lie the writings, published in the late 'forties, of Norbert Wiener and of Claude Shannon, an M.I.T. engineer whose work on "information theory," done in the service of the Bell telephone laboratories, got the machine-linguistic world here excited about things like the probability rules for transmitting "signals" in the presence of "noise." (Shannon's theory and terminology deal specifically with electrical engineering, but they can be applied, at least metaphorically, to just about any "communications" — metaphor being a main thread in the great fabric of communications doctrine now preached in Cambridge.)

After VJ-Day there was lots of interest in machine translation here, and lots of money to support it. At first, in the 'forties, machines were asked only to do simple word-for-word translations, without much allowance for ambiguities of meaning or peculiarities of sentence structure. The results, according to those familiar with them, were barely comprehensible. A young linguist here has told me that he once went through ten pages of such translation and could recognize its subject-matter only because he spotted three key words in it — the rest was a sea of nonsense. And so the linguists, and their backers, soon decided that they were on the wrong track; they came to feel that machine translation, to be useful at all, should be at least as comprehensible as the lowest quality human translation, and they made a start toward achieving this. They have been at it for a decade and a half now, and one gathers they still need several decades more.

In reducing "natural" languages — ordinary human languages, that is — to machine manageability, one must attack and analyze them both semantically (in regard to meaning) and syntactically (in regard to structure). One can begin either way, and so far most of the work here has been done on syntax, for semantics offers problems that may well be tougher — even minor words like "bear," "bit," "bolt," and "brace" have several meanings each; and machines, with their insensitivity to context, cannot easily distinguish between these. Syntax too produces ambiguities: as, for instance, in the sentence "They were eating apples," which can mean — depending on how the structure is understood — either "Those men were eating apples" or "Those apples were destined for eating" (as opposed, say, to cider-making). Professors Miller, Chomsky, Yngve, and Oettinger have discussed this sentence — or its parallel, "They were flying planes" — a good deal. Some of them have also worked on resolving the ambiguities, likewise syntactic, between the verb-senses, noun-senses, and so on of words like "play" in "to play" and "the play," or "green" in "green grass" and "a putting green."

But in addition they have explored some of syntax's deeper mysteries. Chomsky and other linguists have evolved a method of analyzing (or generating) sentences by principles they call "phrase structure" and "transformation."

Under the phrase-structure principle a sentence is seen as made up of simple fragments on which one can operate separately. An elementary sentence in English is likely to consist of a subject and a predicate — a noun-phrase, that is, and a verb-phrase. In generating (or analyzing) such a sentence one may deal first with the earliest part, the noun-phrase — elaborating it and making it specific — while leaving the rest in abeyance. A noun-phrase is likely to consist of a noun preceded by an article; let us take as a specimen phrase "the man." Then we can turn to generating a verb-phrase. A verb-phrase is likely to consist of a verb and an object — a verb, that is, and another noun-phrase. Leaving the noun-phrase in abeyance, let us generate a verb — making it, for instance, "hits." Then finally we may turn to the second noun-phrase; and let us make it "the ball." "The man hits the ball." This way of constructing a sentence is sometimes called a branching method. As frequently diagrammed in Cambridge nowadays it looks like this:

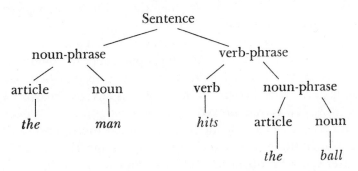

The branching method has the advantage that, so far as possible, you do only one thing at a time with it. While you are working out your subject you leave the rest of the sentence alone; you need only be vaguely aware that a predicate has to be supplied eventually. Psychologists like Miller believe that humans may actually think out the composition of sentences in this way; computer experts like Oettinger and Yngve say that machines can generate sentences relatively well if programmed to use a branching approach; and theoretical linguists like Chomsky believe that "phrase structure" (together with "transformation") gives a true description of a natural language's anatomy. So the scholars are in agreement — "the whole bundle of wax ties together," as one of them puts it.

The branching of a sentence can be far more complex than in the sample given above, and there can be much choice between ways of arranging it. Professor Miller has experimented with the following specimen: "The obviously not very well-dressed man called the people who sold the car that won the race that was held last summer." Tedious as this sentence may be, it is still easy enough to deal with — to read, or repeat, or understand — because the branching is convenient and concentrates on a single idea at a time: first the man, then the calling of the people, then the sale, etc. But Miller has arranged the sentence in another way, also correct grammatically, that goes like this: "The race that the car that the people whom the obviously not very well-dressed man called sold won was held last summer." It is a fright to deal with, as any reader can see and as Miller has proved by experimentation on human subjects. The trouble, he believes, is that there is no relief through successive branchings — that syntactic operation after syntactic operation gets interrupted before it can be disposed of, so the memory is overloaded. The exploration of this process is among the new syntax's contributions to psychology and vice versa — experiments like Miller's, it is believed here, have shed light on grammatical and stylistic points that writers have generally respected in practice, but that have not hitherto been clearly understood. And the work has been most helpful to machine translation — a machine programmed with due regard to branching, Yngve says, can generate far more graceful sentences than were likely a few years ago. At that stage, he explains, machine linguists had become reconciled to awkwardness; they were ready to settle for a good deal of it if they could only get accuracy. But now, thanks to the work done on phrase structure, it looks as if awkwardness would be the least of their worries. Yngve's programs readily generate sentences now like "SHE IS UPHOLSTERED, AND HE IS AFRAID OF THREE NEWSPAPERS" or "A WHISTLE DOESN'T MAKE THE TRUCK GAY, AND SHE SELDOM MAKES WILLITS APPRECIATIVE OF TWO ENGINES EITHER." The sentences are nonsense, because the program takes little account of semantics, but otherwise they seem a fair start toward decent prose.

"Phrase structure" produces declarative sentences — according to the new grammarians — that can then be worked on, and elaborated, by "transformations." "The man hits the ball" can be turned into "The man doesn't hit the ball"; "Does the man hit the ball?"; "The ball is hit by the man"; and so on, right down to "Isn't the ball hit by the man?" where three kinds of transformation — negative, interrogative, and passive — are all present. This phase of syntax has also been under much scrutiny here. Last winter I heard a long and fascinating lecture on "The difficulty of negative statements" given by a young English psychologist who was visiting at Harvard's Center for Cognitive Studies — I believe his talk represented two or three years of research. In the course of this work he had learned — as writers sometimes also learn through prac-

tice — that negative statements can indeed be harder to
deal with than positive ones. This is not a world-shaking
discovery, but in its way it is another addition to the store
of machine-applicable psycho-linguistic knowledge building up here.

Computers are servants that change their masters' lives.
Professor Miller (one of the two entrepreneurs, incidentally, of Harvard's Center for Cognitive Studies) is not
a psychologist prone to confuse men with machines, yet he
is interested in the latter and takes advantage of them in his
research. Recently his center, which enjoys both government and foundation support, invested in a smallish computer for use on its own premises. The computer has a
TV-like screen and also a typewriter keyboard through
which one may converse with it, in writing; and it will have
several duties, according to the center's plans. It will, for
instance, flash numbers briefly before "subjects" and then
after a delay test their memories of them — making tests
by the thousands, with inhuman perseverance, and recording the results. It will also team up closely with a human
investigator in longer-range memory tests — the machine
may ask the questions and record the answers in such tests,
for instance, allowing the human to watch for less routine
occurrences. And then Miller plans some experiments of
his own with certain artificial languages he has been devising. These "languages" have rules that are not explicitly
revealed to the subject of a test — he must learn them,
rather, by trial and error while the machine puts him
through his paces; the aim is to see how easily people can
learn languages through examples alone. When I recently
went to see Dr. Miller — a tall young man with a Mephis-
tophelean beard — he sat me down at the computer's keyboard and let me try a "language" program out. I pressed

a button, and the computer told me to type the letters W, S, and A as many times as I liked and in any order. It so happened that the computer worked badly that day, as machines often do in my presence, but had it worked well it would have scolded "WRONG" whenever I began a string of letters with A, this being a breach of its unstated rules. In time, presumably, I would have learned my lesson — never to start with A — and then the machine would have led me on to other refinements.

One advantage of the computer in this use is its ability (if working well) to spot "grammatical errors" much faster than a human could. A second, in this and other uses at the center, is its lightning facility at recording answers and adding up scores, thus freeing the psychologist for less mechanical work. And a third is the way it can standardize; if a test is programmed onto tape it can be shipped around the country and administered in identical fashion almost anywhere. For reasons like this the computer is becoming for experimental psychologists, as for biophysicists like Professor Rosenblith, a potent laboratory tool. It magnifies their capabilities.

Communication between humans and other humans, through translation, is not the only concern of machine linguists here. Some are also interested in communication between humans and machines, or machines and other machines. Dr. Yngve, the chief of machine translation at M.I.T., has devised a whole man-to-computer language, called COMIT, that differs from other programming "languages" — Fortran, for instance — in being literal or verbal instead of numerical. It may well be the most prevalent non-numerical programming language in the world now, and Yngve's handbook on it has already been translated into French and Italian. COMIT is valuable in Yngve's own operation, for which it was created, because it gives his linguists access to computers by themselves. Yngve's staff is made up, on the whole, of people who are linguists first and computer experts second if at all, and the man-machine interchange has been hard for them. He used to tackle it by teaming up a linguist and a programmer to-gether — the former would ask the latter to work out a program for him; the latter would reply with cross-ques-tions on, say, "What is a noun?"; and the two would be off on a long and tortured conversation. But linguists can handle COMIT unaided, Yngve says, with little extra train-ing. So, it is hoped, can other primarily verbal scholars, and therefore COMIT is expected to help in the forthcoming mass conversion of M.I.T.'s population into computer-users.

Nor are "languages" the only media that will figure in that task, for another crew of M.I.T. wizards has been working out a pictorial — non-notational — man-computer way of exchanging ideas. This enables a man to sketch a design roughly, by electronic means, on a computer's oscil-loscope screen; then to have the computer smooth it out and true it up; then to go on manipulating the design — with man and computer contributing to the work re-ciprocally.

M.I.T. authorities have given me two different explana-tions of the new technique's significance; some say it is aimed mainly at eliminating tedious human draughting-work, others that it has a higher purpose in contributing to a man-machine union, much fuller than the present one, that will be worked out in the next few years. Recently I saw some movies of the technique's use as mere draughts-manship, and I must say this was impressive enough. I saw a wobbly, indiscriminate quadrilateral sketched on the oscilloscope, then saw the computer, on command, square it up into a rectangle. I saw vaguely round silhouettes — they might have belonged to potatoes — sketched on the screen, then saw these become, mysteriously, perfect circles. I saw drawings moved about on the screen, and magnified or reduced in size, all with no more human effort than the waving of a wand. I saw shapes automatically duplicated, again and again, and saw other shapes joined together and fitted — becoming parts of more complex assemblies. And I saw such things done in three-dimensional drawing as well as in two-dimensional. I saw all kinds of manipulations, indeed, so precise and facile that only the technique's great cost, in this experimental stage, seemed to stand between it and the displacement of innumerable draughtsmen.

About the technique's higher uses I must speak less glibly, though I have had the benefit of a long patient explanation from Mr. Douglas Ross, who is in charge of its development (and who previously, in the late 'fifties, led a successful M.I.T. effort in the automation of machine tools — empowering them to make all manner of objects according to instructions punched on tapes). In talking to me Mr. Ross, a youngish man, displayed the visionary fervor that one often finds at M.I.T. He spoke about the variety and the limitations of man-machine languages, and about how pictorial programming could help make up for the latter; he described such programming as dynamic — an expression of changing relationships — and compared it to musical notation, and Arthur Murray's dance language, and the ways in which more complex choreography can be written down. He conjured up exciting thoughts, but left me behind — thanks to my own shortcomings — in visualizing how the whole numerical-verbal-pictorial man-machine communication may work out in future. And I had better drop the subject at this point, noting only that more is to come, undoubtedly, in the integration of computers with academic life here; we may not yet have seen the half of it.

THE GARDEN OF EDUCATION

V I THE NEW TECHNOLOGY, the new money, and the
Cold War have given the professors their new
leverage. But how has education itself been affected? Being
educators themselves, the academics here have developed
strong ideas about their craft and how to improve it. And
being *contemporary* educators — living in a mood of crisis
— they can get their ideas listened to; they can get backing, if their credentials are good; and they have many new
"audio-visual" techniques to play around with. And so the
Cambridge world is in a ferment now, educationally, at all
levels — from the grade schools of the neighborhood,
where new "sophisticated" teaching is tried out, to the
universities themselves, whose methods are in flux. When
I lived here before, Harvard was not much wired up for
sound. She did have a good recorded-poetry collection —
then being installed by its curator, John Sweeney, in a
special room of the new Lamont Library — but she was
still teaching languages by the voice unaided. Now, though,
she has embraced the language-lab idea — she has installed
a big new laboratory, with 36 booths and the latest in

playback-and-recording gear, in the cellar of Boylston Hall, a once seedy old building, now charmingly redecorated, inside the Yard. (Language labs express not only our new technology, incidentally, but also our new globalism, for they favor a practical emphasis on the speaking of foreign languages, for use abroad, instead of the old literary one on the reading of them.)

Meanwhile, as Harvard has changed, M.I.T. has changed still more, in keeping with her nature. Since the 'forties she has broadened her curriculum; she has remodeled her teaching of science and engineering — being helped in the latter by a nine-million-dollar Ford grant; and she has embarked on many technical innovations — she has, for instance, been developing take-home laboratory kits, such as an electronics kit not much bigger than a textbook, with which a student, by tinkering in his room, can learn the secrets of resistors, transistors, capacitors, and diodes, and of "circuitry" involving them.

These innovations affect the Cambridge world itself; but others affecting the world outside are still more noteworthy. Some have been developed in the formal schools of education here — at Harvard or Boston University — but the more striking ones are creations of separate entrepreneurs, men of vision who know what they want to do and how to go about it. In Cambridge these entrepreneurs are usually teachers not of education as such, but of something else. They are reformers from outside the educational bureaucracy.

Their doyen is I. A. Richards, now seventy — a springy-stepping man, with a red face and a mop of near-white hair, who retired in 1963 from teaching at Harvard. Richards, a crusader from an earlier day, seems almost out of place in the new Cambridge. A veteran mountain-climber, he walks the streets here with cap and knapsack. His interests seem donnish, recalling England, where he was born, and Cambridge University, where he began his teaching; in January 1964, he was named a Companion of Honor by Queen Elizabeth. He seems more at home in a discussion of the Greek dramatists than of the latest scientific, or social-scientific, wrinkles in America — he does pepper his conversation with terms from the world of computers and "information theory," but his path into education reform has lain very much through the humanities. In the 1930's, already a well-known critic, he was popularizing Basic English, the creation of C. K. Ogden, with whom he had written a book called *The Meaning of Meaning*. During the Second World War he might have eased off, but by that time he was ensconced at Harvard and absorbed in the problem of teaching second languages, especially English, to beginners (in 1942, he got a big boost from Winston Churchill, who in a surprise speech at Harvard dwelt on Basic English's virtues and those of Richards as its prophet). Since VJ-Day he has continued his language studies, with special attention to new methods. "Technology to the rescue" is his slogan, and through the years he and his collaborator, Christine Gibson, have built up a stock of films, filmstrips, tape-recordings, picture-text combinations, and TV programs — testing and refining them all the while. He argues that these materials — which are easy, of course, to duplicate — could now do the main job of teaching elementary English throughout the world ("the first steps in a language," he says, "can be taught by film better than by any but highly trained and gifted teachers at their best").

With Miss Gibson, Richards has put out a series of books

to teach languages — English, French, Spanish, German, Italian, Russian, Hebrew, Arabic, etc. — through pictures of simple stick-figure humans carrying out actions that are described in a lesson-text. The English version, *English through Pictures,* has already sold more than two million copies, in paperback. Courses of French and Spanish on television, worked up mainly by Miss Gibson, have also been well received. In the 'forties Richards and Miss Gibson founded a non-profit corporation, Language Research Inc., which holds the royalties from their books (together with foundation grants when available) and invests them in new teaching projects and experiments. In 1957, with Ford Foundation backing, Language Research helped set up a closed-circuit TV program in the Chelsea district of Manhattan so as to teach English to the Puerto Ricans there (and Spanish to their neighbors). More recently LR acquired a mobile language lab — a thirty-six-foot trailer with audio-visual gear and booths for eighteen pupils — that is now being used in French-teaching among the public schools of Arlington, a suburb near here.

Professor Richards, who reorganized educational systems in China in the 'thirties, is a widely traveled man obsessed with the need for literacy, right away, among the developing peoples. A lover of English — a poet himself and a professional appreciator of the British poets — he sometimes stresses English, as the second language *par excellence,* to a degree verging on cultural imperialism. Yet English is said to be coming up now almost everywhere — it is the obvious second language for much of Africa and Asia — and the emphasis may not be misplaced. Richards and his staff are currently engaged in a grade-school English-teaching program in Israel, and they have just returned from laying the groundwork for another in Ghana, which may give them a beachhead for wider African operations; like many global reformers here, Richards sees Africa as the great opportunity now. Meanwhile he and Miss Gibson continue to experiment, in an old frame building near the Harvard Yard, with new techniques — even last winter, on the verge of retirement, Richards gave a new seminar at Harvard on visual communication. Though retiring from Harvard itself, he has not retired from Language Research, through which he still propagates his ideas.

A currently more active, and better patronized, entrepreneur of education here is Dr. Jerrold R. Zacharias, a distinguished M.I.T. physicist who got the teaching-reform bug in the 'fifties and has since built up a huge enterprise called Educational Services Incorporated. Zacharias, commonly known as "Zach," is a stocky gray-haired man in his fifties. He came here shortly before Pearl Harbor to work in M.I.T.'s radar project; and later, beginning in 1951, he led in the development of anti-missile defenses at the Lincoln Laboratory. These jobs helped make a name for him in the scientific world, and they also habituated him to the idea of massive assaults — with plenty of manpower and other resources — on critical problems. Back in the Truman Administration, Zach was appointed to what later became the President's Science Advisory Committee. Periodically, he says, this body was briefed on progress being made by the Russians in scientific education, but American education could not be made to speed up competitively. Zach says he got provoked by the anti-intellectual and anti-scientific spirit of the U.S. public. He brooded about it, and in 1956 wrote a memorandum to James R. Killian, Jr., then president of M.I.T., on the teaching of physics in high schools. The next year Russia put her Sputnik into orbit; a cry went up in America about our science teaching; and Zach has been reforming it ever since. His first big achievement, and probably his greatest so far, was the creation of a new high-school physics course. In the past, according to one of Zach's colleagues, most American high-school physics texts were written by high-school physics teachers, which condemned them to mediocrity. But Zach enlisted a team of the best physicists in the country, including two Nobel Prize winners, and got them not only to help in writing new texts, but also to act in movies of experiments and other demonstrations. These films, some of them small masterpieces, are now put out in easily-loaded cartridges and are distributed by commercial agencies along with texts and improved "hardware" for laboratory experiments. Meanwhile books for collateral reading on many aspects of physics are being prepared; Zach's people are editing them and Anchor Books are publishing them, at the rate of nearly one a month. Zach's new course, with all these fittings, has been a great success; it is already being used (at least in part) by a third of the secondary schools in America, including most of the good ones, and many abroad. And since it was launched, Zach's organization has moved on to the reform of our elementary science teaching; to an exploration of new ways to teach the social sciences and humanities here; and to the starting of an ambitious program in Africa.

Zach's activities began under the wing of M.I.T., but as they grew more complex they were "spun off" into Educational Services Inc., a non-profit corporation, with James Killian as chairman of its board, that already occupies space in Cambridge and three buildings and a studio in neighboring Watertown. ESI's history puts it rather in a class with the industrial spin-offs that M.I.T. has generated on Route 128, and Zach also speaks of his work in 128 terms — he says he is engaged in educational "research and development," and he explains that ESI is a natural consequence of his radar and warning-net experiences. He complains that while education in this country is a twenty-five-billion-dollar business, it doesn't spend nearly the percentage of this sum on R & D that an industrial firm would. But still in 1963 ESI spent almost six million dollars, which — as Zach points out with satisfaction — is more than the budget of many a small liberal-arts college.

To a casual observer Zacharias suggests the traditional Hollywood mogul. He seems under a compulsion to dominate the pecking-order. He keeps yes-men within reach;* he holds the floor at all costs; and at meetings of his organization he interrupts his specialists to tell them what they should be saying. Yet he gets things done. He is alert, vital, shrewd, and influential; he is on intimate terms with Killian, Jerome Wiesner, and many other leaders of the new science officialdom — he is, in fact, a leader of it himself — and when he telephones a foundation or government agency his voice is listened to. (Some Cambridge wits talk about a unit of currency called the "zach" — $250,000 — this being, supposedly, the smallest amount Zach thinks it advisable to ask a foundation for.)

Zach's approach to Africa has been typically grandiose. He got interested in that continent while taking part in a conference at Rehovoth, Israel, on the advancement of the underdeveloped areas. During the conference there was

* In ESI, that is. Among his fellow professors, with some of whom he has been serving on a committee to improve the M.I.T. curriculum, he is said to be less dominating. And ESI has also benefited greatly from other gifted teachers who have worked with Zacharias, most notably the late M.I.T. physicist Francis Friedman.

much high-flown talk, annoying to Zach, about things like atomic reactors for such areas, so he was pleased to see the Reverend Solomon Caulker, the vice-prinçipal of a college in Sierra Leone, rise to argue that widespread elementary education, not ultra-sophisticated gadgetry, was what Africa really needed. Thereafter Zach and Caulker took to conversing outside the conference sessions, and in time they agreed to try an African education program. Caulker, it happened, was killed in a plane crash on his way home, but Zach went to work anyway. First he assembled a summer conference, which met for eight weeks (in 1961) at M.I.T.'s baronial Endicott House in Dedham — it was paid for jointly by the Ford Foundation and our foreign-aid program and was attended by twenty Africans, thirty-five Americans, and five third-country experts on African education. They talked and talked, and it was finally decided that ESI should prepare materials for all of English-speaking tropical Africa; should concentrate on the years from kindergarten through the fourteenth grade; and should undertake programs in science, mathematics, and the social-sciences-plus-humanities, with linguistics and teacher-training fitted in somewhere. The math program was chosen as the starter; big interim meetings were held the next winter at Accra, in Ghana, and Ibadan, in Nigeria; and in the summer of 1962 a "workshop" conference of more than fifty experts was assembled for eight weeks at Entebbe, in Uganda, on the shores of Lake Victoria. This conference drafted a first-grade math course and half of an eighth-grade one, which have since been tried out on Africans with considerable success. Meanwhile a second Entebbe conference was held in the summer of 1963 to draft additional math courses, and so it will go.

ESI is not out to push its program down Africa's throat;

it is merely getting up materials — texts and teaching-guides — that the African school systems may use if they wish. No one knows yet what the demand will be, but the Ford Foundation and the U.S.A.I.D. administration (which have been paying, respectively, one-quarter and three-quarters of the program's cost) are gambling that it will be large. Meanwhile ESI is continuing with its efforts at reforming U.S. education and with its sponsorship of the Indian Institute of Technology plus improved engineering instruction at the University of Kabul, in Afghanistan. [These last two ventures are not Zach's creations primarily (see page 110). They were initiated elsewhere and were turned over to ESI for management, on behalf of the consortia of U.S. institutions going in on them.]

Of ESI's later American programs the mathematics one is farthest along; our ideas on math-teaching are especially in flux now, and Zach has some celebrated mathematicians at work on the curriculum. ESI is also developing a new elementary science course that shows much promise, for it can use the talent and techniques — of film-making, etc. — that were brought out in the high-school physics work. There are also two or three smaller, more specialized science programs that are said to be going smoothly. The organization may have its chief trouble, indeed, with the humanities and social sciences, for there it is up against the two-culture problem, in C. P. Snow's phrase, or even a three-culture problem — the social sciences pursue a rather separate course in Cambridge, and have done so at least since the late 'forties, when they became especially prominent at Harvard with the setting up there of a new Department of Social Relations. Since then (at least) the humanities have frowned somewhat on the social sciences because of their often grotesque English and their tendency to invade the realm of fiction and the other arts. The physical sciences, too, have looked on them with a certain pity because of their struggle to deal scientifically with concepts not amenable to laboratory verification. Zach himself shows some of this condescension; he speaks of wanting to endow the social scientists with the "dignity of having a laboratory," and he emphasizes the introduction of "hardware" into his social-science course. This idea sounds promising when the subject is the Eskimos and other primitive peoples, with whom artifacts are so important (and who are being handled for ESI, incidentally, by an able anthropologist), but it sounds less so when the subject is history, for then the hardware is apt to come down to mere photostats of documents that the children can play around with. As for the humanities, ESI has shown even less of a green thumb with them so far. In neighboring Harvard, after all, it has one of the greatest humanities mills ever known, yet few Harvard professors have grown excited over the ESI humanities program. Even so Zach can certainly make a try at reforming the field. In 1963 he got the better part of a million dollars from the Ford Foundation on which he can draw for the purpose, and there is presumably more where that came from. America, for a scholar-innovator of Zach's ability, is very much a land of promise now.

Among the dozens of experts working with Zach there is one, the Harvard psychologist Jerome Bruner, who is a considerable entrepreneur in his own right. A charming, well-dressed, articulate man in his late forties — with extra-thick glasses and a well-domed, baldish Cambridge head — Bruner is a partner with his colleague George Miller in running the Harvard Center for Cognitive Studies. Much of his time there, and that of his students and assistants, is spent on research into the learning process; they use children in the local schools as subjects, and recently the center acquired a $35,000 mobile laboratory (financed by the U.S. government along with Harvard) to help make this work more efficient — eventually, Bruner plans, the laboratory will also travel to Africa, for use in "cross-cultural" research on children there.

Bruner is aiming, he says, at providing the basis for a theory of instruction. He is studying how the arrangement of a child's "exposure to the environment" can lead to the growth of its understanding; in this he experiments with the extension of children's vocabularies, for instance, and with their ability to grasp algebraic operations through being led into equivalent manipulations of building-blocks or balancing-scales. Bruner's theories are not fully crystallized yet, and they may be far better known in the future than at present, but he is already looked on as very much a coming man here. He is a prolific and influential writer, he is one of ESI's chief idea-men, and last June he even ran a rather Zach-like conference of his own in Cambridge, for two weeks, on teaching theory (it was paid for by the government). Recently the magazine *Pageant* — saying that Bruner's ideas are the "most talked about" in education since John Dewey — listed him as one of the "ten Americans to watch in 1963."

Meanwhile, one hears even more about another Harvard psychologist-educator, B. Frederic Skinner, the developer of "programmed instruction" or the teaching-machine. Skinner — who likewise wears the standard local facade of spectacles, a soaring brow, and receding hair — is a man of delicate mien, and a graceful writer on many subjects. He is a "behaviorist" whose education theories are derived

from studying pigeons and who finds himself in disagree-
ment with Drs. Bruner, Zacharias, Richards, and many
others in the community. As a behaviorist he believes that
all thought processes are revealed in action, which leads
him to rule out some of Bruner's theorizing. And as a
pigeon-trainer he believes that trainees should be rewarded
or encouraged only *after* they have done something desirable, which leads him to dismiss audio-visual aids as
pleasurable excitements administered too soon. The sweet-
ening of educational pills through entertainment, he says,
only produces candy addicts — "four-color illustrations
don't teach a child to read; they make him a customer for
Look, Life and the comics." And so Skinner's movement
stands apart from the other educational ones here, though
he himself is generally on good terms with their leaders.
He and Richards are friends, but they engage in sharp
combat. They debate sometimes in polemical verse — an
exchange of theirs was recently published in the British
magazine *Encounter* — and once when Skinner was invited
to address a Richards class, he says, Richards introduced
him by saying "This is the Devil," and then sat down.

Skinner's work stems in part from Pavlov's experiments
on the conditioned reflexes of dogs. Skinner himself began
working with rats three decades ago, then later switched to
pigeons. He taught them by "reinforcing" desirable actions
in them with rewards of corn. If he wanted a pigeon to peck
an object that lay to its right, say, he would give it a grain
of corn when it turned its head in that direction, however
slightly, and thus gradually he would lead it on. In this
way he taught pigeons to distinguish playing cards, to peck
out tunes on a toy piano, to play a sort of table tennis, and
to do many other things. During the Second World War he
even devised a system for the guiding of missiles by pigeons.

In this he taught each pigeon to single out the image of a chosen target, in an aerial photograph, and to peck at it. Meanwhile he and his colleagues designed a pigeon-chamber to go in a missile's nose. There a pigeon would stand, according to the plan — or rather three pigeons would stand, to make assurance triply sure — while they sped through the sky toward a scene familiar to them from their photograph-training. They would see this scene through a transparency and would dutifully peck at the target in it. If the target showed in the center they would peck there, and the missile would hold to its course, but if it showed to one side or above or below they would peck *there* and cause the guidance system, by electrical means, to make an adjustment. Skinner claims he had the guidance problem solved in this way, but unfortunately the military — because, he thinks, of a prejudice favoring inanimate contraptions against animate ones — dropped the scheme after a brief moment of supporting it.

In his programmed teaching Skinner treats humans like pigeons in that he "reinforces" desirable acts on their part — not by giving them corn, but by letting them know that they are right; he teaches by asking questions, and the reinforcement is the confirmation of the answers. A program of his may include dozens of such questions, each leading on to another and another and another, in a carefully planned sequence. Hints are freely given in a well-designed program, and the student is nudged into making right answers almost in spite of himself. Here is the beginning of a program in high-school physics.

1. The important parts of a flashlight are the battery and the bulb. When we "turn on" a flashlight, we close a switch which connects the battery with the _____.

2. When we turn on a flashlight, an electric current flows through the fine wire in the _____ and causes it to grow hot.

3. When the hot wire glows brightly, we say that it gives off or sends out heat and _____.

4. The fine wire in the bulb is called a filament. The bulb "lights up" when the filament is heated by the passage of a(n) _____ current.

5. When a weak battery produces little current, the fine wire, or _____, does not get very hot.

6. A filament which is *less* hot sends out or gives off _____ light.

7. "Emit" means "send out." The amount of light sent out, or "emitted," by a filament depends on how _____ the filament is.

It is clear, even in so brief a fragment, that new ideas are introduced very gently; the word "filament" is withheld, for instance, until the pupil is deemed ready for it, and meanwhile "fine wire" is used as a stand-in. Likewise "emit" is withheld for a while. Then later in this same lesson, new concepts of "incandescence," "energy," and so on are introduced with equal subtlety, and meanwhile earlier ideas like that of "filament" are gone over again. Skinner programs are conveyed to students either by teaching-machines — of which several models, more or less the size of a typewriter, are being made now — or else by books or loose sheets. With a proper machine the pupil first writes out his answer and then pulls a lever, or turns a knob, that moves this writing out of sight — so he can't change it — while at the same time revealing the correct answer along with the next question. In this way three good effects are produced, according to Skinner's disciples: the pupil is forced to make a clear decision; he has the satis-

faction of acting on it; and he has the added satisfaction of
learning that he is right (in the Skinner view a good program makes wrong answers virtually impossible).

Skinner argues that John Dewey put teaching at a disadvantage by taking the coercion out of it without replac-
ing it by anything — he thinks this end of coercion was a
good thing, but feels that it left a vacuum of incentive. As
we have noted, he doesn't think the vacuum can be filled
by interesting or exciting presentations of the audio-visual
sort; he believes the job can be done only by his own system,
which he considers a natural one. His critics here object
strongly to his system, saying that it is too mechanical; that
it disregards the pupil-teacher relationship; and that its
slowness and repetitiveness, to the end of making all questions easy, are merely boring. Whether these charges are
valid or not, Skinner's programs *have* made some impressive records; bright students have learned subjects through
teaching-machines, and learned them retentively, in a fraction of the time it would have taken them otherwise. One
strong point of the system, of course, is that it lets a good
student forge ahead independently, without waiting for
duller classmates; and such independence is useful in other
ways too — teaching-machines can be used at home, and
when used in schools they can help relieve the teacher
shortage, or can free teachers for lecturing and consulta-
tion.

Partly because of its flexibility, programmed instruction
is in demand in business and industry; insurance and other
companies are using programs to teach routine procedures
to their employees. There is money in programming, and
it has been taken up in a commercial way; most of the
several hundred courses so far devised have been put out
by business firms, of which dozens are engaged in the line

now, a few of them located in or near Cambridge. Skinner has sometimes worked as a consultant with these firms, but for the most part he has turned their offers down. He says he is too engrossed in writing and research, and also that American business does not do the right kind of job with programming. One trouble, he maintains, is that even bad programs are effective, and so all manner of crudely-thought-out ones are on the market — also crudely-presented ones in, say, book form (though books can print answers upside down, and put them on pages separate from the questions, they can't really prevent peeking, or the lazy reading of a program; they lack a machine's strictness in forcing honest pigeon-like actions from a pupil). If Skinner was at M.I.T. — with its closer ties to business and fuller acceptance of the business outlook — he might conceivably be a tycoon now of teaching-machines, with a plant on 128 and a staff of experts writing programs for him. But in fact he is a withdrawn scholar at Harvard, and withdrawing even from there; at age fifty-five he is cutting down on his teaching now and turning more toward writing and perhaps toward participation in a utopian community, which is an idea that interests him. Meanwhile, though, some of his disciples — the senior one being Dr. James G. Holland — are carrying on his programming work at a small center, backed by the Carnegie Corporation, here in Cambridge. They are experimenting at the center, are devising new programs, and are instructing teachers who come to visit from other parts of the country. And so the movement, with or without its founder, goes on as a semi-academic enterprise.

The hospital world of Boston is closely linked to Cambridge and has been going through a renaissance of late with the same elements of globalism, outside money, new technology, and new centers of activity. This world consists mainly of the Harvard, Tufts, and B.U. medical schools and the hospitals co-operating with them; its greatest part is the Harvard Medical Center, made up of seven teaching hospitals together with the Harvard Schools of Medicine, and Dental Medicine. Then there is the Harvard School of Public Health. I have a friend at M.I.T. who blames it for the worldwide population explosion. "People from the school," he said recently, "are coming and going everywhere, combatting mass mortality. They travel through Latin America, fighting tropical diseases, and they are cleaning up trachoma, you know, the great source of blindness in the Middle East. A Harvard task-force, backed by the Arabian-American Oil Company, has just isolated the trachoma virus, and is working out a vaccine now. That has hardly been dreamed of before, in trachoma's thousands of years of history." My friend didn't say so, but another team from the School flew recently to New Delhi, to see about starting an institute for family planning there — a move *against* the population explosion. And these ventures are just samples; doctors from the School of Public Health, and from the Harvard Medical School as well, are in orbit all the time now. (And foreigners keep flying this way too, coming to the great center to be healed; Ibn Saud and Anthony Eden are recent examples.)

Just before the Second World War the Harvard Medical School was getting 2 per cent of its support from the Federal government, and now it is getting almost 60 per cent. In the school year 1960–61 this Federal contribution came to six million dollars, in grants for research and training, and it was divided among no less than twenty-five hundred people. Nor are government grants the whole thing. Much money comes from private industry — like the Aramco expenditure on trachoma — and from foundations and endowments.

The interaction between Harvard and M.I.T. is evident in this field, too. For instance, there is the odd history of a device worked out at M.I.T. for use in Polaris missiles, which was later found valuable in measuring the viscosity of blood; a Harvard doctor is now using the device in vascular studies, related to things like clotting and arteriosclerosis. There is also the use of proton beams, generated at the Harvard cyclotron, in treating — successfully, for the first time anywhere — brain tumors and diabetes. And then there is Walter Rosenblith's computer technique for studying the nervous system, which is being applied clinically with cases of deafness in newborn babies. Nor, again, is that the end of it; the proximity of medicine to technology here has led to teamwork of all sorts.

Of centers and entrepreneurs, finally, we need cite only a few. The Harvard School of Public Health has a brand-new Guggenheim Center for Aerospace Health and Safety, headed by Professor Ross McFarland, which will study things like the effect on humans of weightlessness. And the School has a still newer Center for Population Studies, just forming up, which is *another* move against the population explosion, this time at the home base. (Its work is in addition to that of Dr. John Rock, the great contraceptives expert, who has just retired from Harvard and is ensconced in a center of his own in nearby Brookline.)

One cannot discuss the medical renaissance without mentioning the researches of Drs. John F. Enders and Thomas H. Weller, the Harvard Nobel Prize winners whose studies, along with those of Frederic C. Robbins, of Western Reserve, lie behind the polio vaccines and who have more recently isolated the measles virus (German and regular) and developed a vaccine for *it*. And to go back across the Charles, to Cambridge and the biologists at Harvard, one must mention one especially: Dr. James D. Watson, who got a Nobel Prize in 1962 (with two British scientists) for working out the structure of the DNA molecule. This feat has inspired all kinds of experiments, and much of the biological research throughout the world now stems from it. DNA controls protein synthesis, in current belief, and hence heredity. Therefore the follow-ups to Watson's discovery, eagerly pursued in Cambridge as elsewhere, are expected to yield great news about life and perhaps great means of influencing it. One often hears it said now, in Cambridge scientific circles, that physics has had its day of excitement — that the big discoveries are over, and a time of refinement has set in — and that meanwhile molecular biology will be the great thing in the next few decades. That means Watson's work, and what comes out of it. It is all part of the Cambridge boom.

It is with reason that Cambridge's Mayor Crane has called his city a "garden of architecture." The architecture here is really both a setting for the new age and a part of that age. It is very global, for one thing. "People all over the world look to Cambridge," a young friend in the profession told me the other day. "Some of the world's greatest architects have settled here. Pietro Belluschi, the dean of the School of Architecture and Planning at M.I.T., is an Italian. José Luis Sert, the dean of Harvard's Faculty of Design, is a Spaniard originally — a European at large since the Spanish War — and Walter Gropius, formerly chairman of the Department of Architecture, who still lives here, is a German. Many on their faculties are foreigners

too, like the Hungarian Gyorgy Kepes, at M.I.T. Then
other famous foreigners — the Pole Jerzy Soltan, for instance, and the Swiss architectural historian Sigfried Gie-
dion — have been coming here to teach intermittently.
Foreigners have also designed many buildings in Cambridge. The Finns Alvar Aalto and Eero Saarinen are represented by very good work at M.I.T., and Le Corbusier's
only building in North America is the new Carpenter
Center for the Visual Arts at Harvard, which is a fine example of his later, concrete-sculptural style — if nothing
else, it will always be a museum-piece for Cambridge, of
twentieth-century international architecture. There are
other such monuments as well, for Sert and Gropius, to
name only two, have been leaving their mark on the town.
Harvard's graduate-school dormitory quadrangle, designed
by Gropius's firm, is inspired by the Bauhaus style he
helped to develop in Germany, during the 'twenties and
early 'thirties."

Influences going out to the world from Cambridge, my
friend told me, are just as important as those coming in;
they go out through the many foreign architectural students graduating from Harvard and M.I.T., and also
through the global operations of private firms here, especially the Gropius firm — called The Architects Collab-
orative, or TAC — which is doing several jobs in Europe,
Asia, and Africa. TAC specializes in school and college
design, my friend said. "Architecture has grown so complex technologically," he explained, "that it is hard for a
firm to do the old kind of diversified practice — today on
a single job you may have a stack of blueprints several
inches thick, where once you had just a few sheets — and
many firms, therefore, have stopped trying to know everything. Instead they pick out a specialty, and TAC's is edu-

cational building. Cambridge is a good place to pursue it, what with the Harvard School of Education right at hand and the new audio-visual and teaching-machine techniques — both of which need architectural aids such as pupils' booths — being worked out here. TAC has done jobs recently at Brandeis and Harvard, but above all it has designed new primary- and secondary-school buildings — dozens of them — in New England and other parts of America. Abroad, Gropius has done some non-educational work — he designed the new American embassy in Athens — but again schools have been his main work. The firm has been designing them, or helping to design them, in Nigeria, Guinea, and Mali. TAC is also working on a big university in Tunis and on another in Baghdad."

Other firms here are doing foreign business, too — on a lesser scale, perhaps, but still one hears of great prosperity among the leading local architects. And Cambridge has a more institutional global link as well: the Joint Center for Urban Studies, which is backed by the Ford Foundation and affiliated with both Harvard and M.I.T., signed a contract in 1960 with a Venezuelan government agency to work out a "development strategy" for the Guayana region on the Orinoco. The region is potentially rich — it has been called the "future Ruhr of South America" — and is getting the benefit of such new installations as a steel-mill and a system of dams. A new city of perhaps half a million, called Santo Tomé de Guayana, is envisioned, and it has a population of sixty thousand already. The development is being run by Venezuelans, with the Joint Center here doing much of the basic theoretical work as a consultant — the Center would like to have other jobs in underdeveloped countries too, "development" being one of its research specialties, along with studies in urban design, urban trans-

portation, and the rapid growth of cities in modern times.
(This center is remarkable, as Cambridge centers go, in
being a joint enterprise, and also for its double emphasis
on research and practical application — i.e., planning under
contract.) It was started, incidentally, only in 1959. Its
original entrepreneur was Martin Meyerson, professor of
planning at Harvard, but he left in 1963 to become dean
of the School of Environmental Design at the University
of California. His successor is James Q. Wilson of the Harvard Department of Government.

Technology plays its part, of course, in the architectural
boom at Cambridge, and my young friend has explained
this to me also. "In Cambridge you are in the mainstream
of innovation," he said recently. "There is no other place
like it. You have people here like Albert Dietz, professor
of civil engineering and architecture at M.I.T., who is
probably the world's foremost expert on the use of plastics
in building — the Monsanto plastic house, you know, was
done at M.I.T. Then great studies on the modular aspect
of building have been made at the Institute, too, in the
Albert Farwell Bemis Foundation there; the Cambridge
architect Carl Koch has drawn on those studies for his
Techbuilt houses, which are designed here and sold all
over the country. M.I.T. also leads in acoustical research,
and the Cambridge firm of Bolt, Beranek & Newman — all
of whose partners teach at M.I.T. — is the world's leading
acoustical consultant. Buckminster Fuller does part of his
research and development in Cambridge too; his firm Geo-
desics, Inc., has offices right near Harvard Square. Cambridge really is the center now, for the spawning of new
techniques."

When viewed primarily as a setting for the Cambridge

renaissance, instead of a product thereof, the new architecture here is remarkable chiefly for its verticality and its addiction to concrete. High-rise buildings have been going up this year on all three big campuses along the Charles — those of Harvard, M.I.T., and Boston University — with more still on the drafting-boards. They threaten to give Charles-side architecture a uniformity it has lacked. Harvard once presented, to the Charles, a row of red-brick Georgian facades almost without interruption. M.I.T. had a long, low — very horizontal — cream-colored neoclassical aspect. And B.U., a big struggling "commuter" institution — midway between the other two, on the facing bank — was ensconced in a hodgepodge that included many old riverside houses of the brownstone era. Now, though, each campus has gray skyscrapers, twenty stories high or more, going up from it like towers. They are needed to house married students, or new interdisciplinary centers, or additions of some other sort, and the expansion is vertical because the universities want to keep tight perimeters, for the sake of unity, without sacrificing any more open space than they have to. Also, of course, because land outside the perimeters is expensive, and its acquisition by these tax-free institutions often arouses the town-and-gown hostility. (Some observers here maintain that the great local universities might have lost more of their tax-freeness already if it weren't for the nearby presence of Cardinal Cushing and the enterprises of his diocese, which benefit from the same thing.)

The prevalence of concrete in the new Cambridge is closely associated with the name of José Luis Sert, the Harvard dean, whose firm — Sert, Jackson & Gourley* — has been designing buildings for B.U. as well as for Har-

* Gourley recently left the firm and is now on his own in Cambridge.

vard itself. Harvard's student daily, the *Crimson,* saluted
the change last spring by quoting an old ditty:

> In sixteen hundred, thirty-six,
> Harvard College was built of bricks.

— and then suggesting some new lines for the future:

> By nineteen hundred, eighty-four,
> Those bricks of red were seen no more.
> With José Luis Sert's ascent,
> They changed the bricks to cold cement.

The *Crimson* went on to attack the Sert buildings as
"Incinerator Gothic" — a not very apt term — and to char-
acterize them generally as "ugly, menacing, stark and big."
In future years the main objection to these buildings may
be that there are too many of them too much alike — too
many surfaces of coarse concrete relieved almost frantically
by touches of bright color and by baffles, balconies, arcades,
ledges, corrugations, and other roughnesses protruding
from them.*

There is also a lack of privacy in some new Cambridge
buildings that conflicts with the scholarly need for concentration. Modern architects are so infatuated with light
and space, perhaps, that they can't see this need for seclu-
sion — also, of course, they have before them the horrid
examples of dingy Gothic quadrangles built at Yale and
other places a few decades ago. But Georgian isn't dingy. I
lived in Harvard Georgian quarters for a few months in
1963, and I found peace and quiet there with light and
spaciousness as well. Some of the newer anti-traditional
buildings here don't score so high. Gropius's graduate-
school dormitories are partitioned with walls of cinder

* But see page 83.

blocks, and one hears that the tiniest noise carries through. Le Corbusier's Visual Arts Center is so glassy that it is hard to heat and is open to many distractions for both eye and ear. It also has some brightly colored inner surfaces whose reflections tend to confuse the visual arts being practiced. I have a friend who gives a seminar on the center's top floor, in a smallish room beneath a skylight whose deep inset is painted a brilliant red. I was visiting him there one day, and he began telling me about the place. He had been having trouble, he said, with the shadows of passing clouds and planes, which often flitted across the seminar table with almost shattering effect on the deliberations.

"And what about that red?" I asked, pointing up at the skylight-inset. "Isn't it hard to deal with color under it?"

"You almost can't," he answered, shaking his head. "You almost can't."

Brandeis too has its share of distraction-traps, including plate-glass in some buildings between halls and classrooms, or between halls and teachers' offices, so that trains of thought are broken by the passage of pretty co-eds. And the place's library has similar weaknesses. But Brandeis is a special case anyway. It has been built almost wholly in the past fifteen years under a leadership not well experienced with campus architecture or with architecture of any kind in rustic surroundings (the site is in wooded hills outside of suburban Waltham). Not surprisingly, under the circumstances, mistakes have been made — certain buildings have been crowded together, for instance, in an unnecessarily urban way. Even so, the pleasures of Brandeis architecture far outweigh the pains; the campus is already a good museum of twentieth-century work, and is getting better all the time. It is a fitting part of this strange, and strangely influential, new community of Cambridge.

Influential with the world, that is, and with the nation, but whether influential with Greater Boston, its own immediate neighborhood, is another question. To a remarkable degree the Cambridge academics are in that neighborhood, but not of it. They like the Boston cultural events — the theaters, concerts, and exhibitions — and these things, without much doubt, are among the attractions that bring them to the universities here, or to the firms on Route 128. But they don't especially like Boston to live in; they prefer Cambridge itself or the Middlesex villages out northwest of here — like Belmont, Lexington, and Concord — in the Paul Revere direction. They don't like the Boston papers either; many read the New York *Times* instead. And their relationship to Boston and Cambridge politics is singular. They talk about them all the time — about their corruption — but with few exceptions they do little to improve them. The last Cambridge academic who ran for office in a big way was H. Stuart Hughes, professor of history at Harvard, in 1962. Hughes started at the top — running for the Senate, as an independent, without proving himself in lower posts first — and he had a platform, built round the advocacy of nuclear disarmament, that was bound to lose. He got few votes from the multitude, but he did offer his fellow Cambridge intellectuals a way out of a bad predicament: many hated to vote for Ted Kennedy, who was allied to Boston politics and besides was one Kennedy too many; they also hated to vote for Kennedy's main rival, George Lodge, because he was a Republican; and they hated not to vote at all, because they saw voting as a duty. And so they were able to vote for Hughes and remain true to academic withdrawal.

This "lack of communication" between Academe and the surrounding culture has many aspects. Boston is undergoing a huge redevelopment program, for instance — being ploughed up and rebuilt in all directions. A few Cambridge designers, including Koch, Sasaki, Belluschi, and TAC, have individual jobs in connection with this vast work, but the overall Cambridge planning talent has not; the Joint Center for Urban Studies would no doubt have liked very much to get in on it, but has found Venezuela more approachable. And there is virtually no social fraternizing between the academics here and the neighboring masses. The former believe theoretically in equality — in all men being brothers — yet most of them in fact are leading well-fed, well-housed middle-class lives quite different from those of the Greater Boston poor, whom they exclude from close proximity by traditional means; some of the good Cambridge houses adjoining the slums of Somerville even have backyard fences that look like stockades of the Indian days. They form an intercultural pale.

Regardless of theory, then, the Cambridge Academe is not much good at getting on with its immediate neighbors. But getting on with the world is something else. "I don't understand it," a European refugee professor said here the other day. "I was brought up partly in Paris — I went to the Sorbonne among other things. I could easily see then why Paris was a great center. All those roads had been planned that way, by all those Louis. You had to follow them and Paris was where they led to. But Cambridge isn't that way at all. Nobody planned roads leading here that I can see. And yet Cambridge is a great center, as great, perhaps, as any in the world now. It has a strange magnetism." The professor shrugged. "I can't understand that magnetism," he repeated, "but still I feel it. That's why I'm here." And raising his eyebrows, he gazed out at the Charles.

INDEX